Testimony

Testimony: A Life in Poetry

First edition © 2015 The Lontar Foundation
Copyright for all English-language translations by their respective translators
Publication data for the poems may be found in the back of the book

Publication of the Modern Library of Indonesia Series, of which this book is one title,
has been made possible by the generous assistance of The Djarum Foundation.
Funding for the translation of this book was provided by
the Indonesian Translation Funding Program
of the Ministry of Education and Culture, the Republic of Indonesia.

Template design by DesignLab; layout and cover by Cyprianus Jaya Napiun
Cover illustration detail from S Teddy D,
Seri Kepala Baru 3 (New Head Series 3)

Printed in Indonesia by PT Suburmitra Grafistama

ISBN No. 978-602-9144-39-0

MODERN LIBRARY OF INDONESIA

RENDRA

Testimony

A Life in Poetry

Selected by
Edi Haryono

Translations by
Harry Aveling
Burton Raffel
John H McGlynn

Introduction by
Harry Aveling

Jakarta, Indonesia

Contents

Introduction

Rendra (1935–2009) was both a great Indonesian poet and a great man of the theater: an actor, director and scriptwriter. As Burton Raffel wrote: "Rendra is a dramatist, in some broad meanings of that word: there is drama in virtually everything he does and, equally naturally, everything he does tends to find its way into his poetry" (1974: 258).

Rendra was the author of thirteen volumes of poetry, beginning with *Ballada Orang-Orang Tercinta* (Ballads of the Beloved Ones, 1957) and *Empat Kumpulan Sajak* (Four Collections of Verse, 1961), through to *Perjalanan Bu Aminah* (Mother Aminah's Journey, 1997) and *Doa untuk Anak Cucu* (Prayers for My Grandchildren), which appeared posthumously in 2013. His plays include *Orang-Orang di Tikungan Jalan* (People at the Corner of the Road, 1954), *Mastodon dan Burung Condor* (The Mastodon and the Condors, 1972), *Kisah Perjuangan Suku Naga* (Struggle of the Naga Tribe, 1975), *SEKDA* (The Governor's Secretary, 1977) and *Panembahan Reso* (Lord Reso, 1986), as well as many translations of European plays such as *Oedipus Rex*, *Waiting for Godot*, *Hamlet*, *Macbeth*, *Antigone* and *The Caucasian Chalk Circle*. Much of his poetry and theater work was controversial and brought him into conflict with government authorities. He was arrested several times during the 1970s and imprisoned for five months in 1978, after a poetry reading at the Jakarta Arts Center, allegedly because of the potential threat he posed to "public security". Following his release, he found it extremely difficult for most of the next decade to either present his dramatic productions or recite his poetry in public.

This book contains works from all of Rendra's thirteen volumes of poetry. His style is remarkably consistent throughout. Raffel describes his poetry as "long-limbed free verse", in which "the original does not rhyme, has no fixed number of words per line, and has no fixed number of lines per strophe". It is, as a consequence, "an extraordinarily flexible instrument" (Raffel 1967: 171). The subject matter is also consistent. These are, on the whole, narratives of human life: of love, suffering, social injustice, and death.

Some of the poems are personal. Rendra accepted emotion for what it is and gloried in it. He was proud of being human and proud of being male. As a young man, he enjoyed living in Yogyakarta and relying on "the leaves, mountains and river water" (Rendra, cited Raffel 1967: 171). In response to his first two books, *Ballada Orang-Orang Tercinta* and *Empat Kumpulan Sajak*, Rendra was commonly seen by critics as: "a child of nature, completely aware of his naturalness… happily involved with nature… enjoying its beauty and the beauty of his own heart" (Trisno Sumardjo 1962). Certainly this was true for much of the poetry written around the time of his marriage in 1959 to Clara Theresia Sunarti Suwandi (named in the poem "Love Letter" simply as "Dik Narti", little sister Narti; although as Raffel notes, this is "an unsatisfactory translation of *adik*, 'little sister', used also for a wife, a sweetheart, and as a form of address for younger people generally". He continues: "Rendra himself, whose English is good, wishes that the word had been translated here as 'darling', but the English poem that the translation attempts to be could not survive such a rendering" (Raffel 1967: 176).)

Often, however, Rendra used nature not for its own sake but to reinforce the emotional effects he sought in his central narratives. In "Love Letter", the rain "drizzles like a toy/ drum", "the wind sighs" and "two small wild ducks/ are making love in the pond/ like two naughty children/ funny and nice". Nature here reflects the happiness of the forthcoming marriage. But it can also reflect pain and suffering. In the grotesque "Ballad of Kasan and Patima", to take an opposite example, the moon is a pale sickly green, the witch Patima casts her spells from a graveyard in the middle of the night, the trees are bare like her boney fingers, and Kasan flees from her curse under the cover of darkness, only to be "hurled down the Southern Mountain, on the rocky soil", and swallowed by "the pitch-black night", together with his wife and children.

The major dimension of his poetry is not personal in the conventional literary sense; there is little deep psychological self-analysis or philosophical enquiry, and certainly no irony or understatement. Rendra's poetic testimony largely relied on the telling of stories, about himself and the world around him. Many of his poems are "ballads", as he called the earlier poems, or narratives concentrating on the social outsider, "poems" as he categorized the majority of his later work. The stories deal with "the underdogs… the victims, the solitary, the eccentrics", and in the beginning, they are "nearly always people from the villages" (Teeuw 1967: 233). The outsider in Rendra's poems is often a criminal, a man of violence, a thief, sometimes a soldier, or a grieving woman. But the outsider may also be a poor person, an older person, a child, or someone rejected by someone else. To be deprived of the opportunity to live a basic life, to lack love and compassion, is already to be an outsider. In the poems, we watch the action work itself out through deed and dialogue into some definitive resolution. Sometimes this narrative is accompanied by a chorus that slowly changes in response to the unfolding of the narration. It is the essence of the drama presented in Rendra's poetry that the action is graphic and inescapable, the men strong and the women suffering, and that death is ultimately the master of all.

Following his studies at the American Academy of Dramatic Arts in New York, 1964-1967, a change occurred in Rendra's writing as seen in *Blues untuk Bonnie* (Blues for Bonnie, 1971: from page 65 on in this volume). His language became simplified, less reliant on colorful images, more direct and harsher, not far removed (in many people's eyes) from the language of the press. Importantly, many of Rendra's poems were set increasingly in the city. The city is an American city in some poems: New York or Boston, as in "For MG", "Rick from

Corona" and "Blues for Bonnie". These are places of casual and meaningless contact between isolated individuals. In other poems, the city is Indonesian and social relations are more hierarchical, more based on the use of force and have long lasting effects. They are also inescapable. In both cases, the dominant note is that of the cruel indifference: of mankind to nature, and of people to other people.

A religious dimension to suffering quickly became clear in Rendra's early poetry. Rendra was born a Catholic and raised within a broad Javanese mystical milieu. As he approached his middle twenties, he began to explore new metaphors to describe God and His presence in the world. At first the images were positive and reinforced the perception of Rendra as a man close to nature. In "Morning Psalm", for example, the light in the mountains is God setting His "beautiful body" down, and "Ducks lay eggs/ at the touch of Your hand./ Fish leap in the water/ and the rice stalks wave/ greeting You". The God of "Evening Prayer" is an "incomparable Magician", with "phosphorescent hands", who allows the poet's child to "sleep in Your pocket" and his wife to "sail in Your blood". "Multicolored paper flowers" scatter from His mouth, and He promises to have "other magic tricks" tomorrow. These images of God interacting with nature then quickly became pantheistic and humanized. "Rose Psalm" described God as "a wounded soldier", "a wise old man/in torn clothing", a friend and neighbor of "thieves, bandits/ and murderers" as well as of adulterers, but also "a dusty gambling table/ pelted with cards", and even "worms for geese and pigs to eat". God was in everything and everyone, in good and evil alike.

This identification of God and suffering humanity was also applied to Christ. "A Saint" is described in the poem of that name as "a man who sins/ and always rises again". He is a frail sick man, "a meddler" who liked to help people, "a stupid man from a drought stricken village", the father of three indifferent children, who is "crucified" by the sins of the world, and dies "with both arms outstretched". The poems written in America took these established images into distinctly more radical directions. In "Swan Song", the dying prostitute,

Maria Zaitun, meets and makes love to a handsome young man, who has scars in his side, his hands and feet. A Catholic, she knows whom he is and he confirms her understanding. A young priest, in "Sermon", is attacked by his congregation, raped, and his flesh and blood consumed in a joyful feast. These images can conceivably be fitted into certain types of orthodox readings. Christ cared for the poor and His disciples included Mary Magdelene, a prostitute. A priest is a consecrated representative of Christ and gives his life for his people. This comfortable orthodoxy was not Rendra's intention. With these images came a rejection of the Church: on her journey to death, Maria Zaitun met with a priest who was finishing his long lunch and he refused to hear her confession or to show her any pity. Christ accepts her: the priest and "the angel who guards paradise" did not. The congregation feast on the body and blood of the priest, a representative of Christ, but it is a cannibalistic orgy, conducted to a steady "cha-cha" beat, rather than a "holy Communion". God was now to be found outside the Church; the holy company of the saints consists of the dispossessed and the wretched. (Rendra converted to Islam in late 1970 and took a second wife. He took a third wife in 1976.)

Rendra's early ballads were like folk tales in which the social background was largely irrelevant. The poems produced by his American experiences became more conscious of wider social contexts. They also became more critical. When the religious influence diminished, a simple moral philosophy came to explicitly underpin Rendra's view of society. It was that all are human, and that respectability and immorality are arbitrary social judgments. In the assessment of "An Angry World": "Avoiding death/ is their main problem/ not welfare or sin./ How can they understand the voice of heaven/ if they have never heard the voice of life?" Most of the outsiders are powerless victims of their circumstances. On the other hand, the respectable are, because of their lack of compassion, hypocrites, acting out on a grand scale and with impunity the same crimes for which the poor are punished severely. "The Pickpocket's

Advice to his Mistress" was precisely that she should imitate her lover, a senior government figure: steal, lie, cheat, make provision for her own future, and have no regard for anyone else. The "prostitutes of Jakarta" should "unite" simply because they were being persecuted by the same government that relied on their services and refused to make them an honest recompense. (In a speech in 2001, Rendra argued that "Without compensation there cannot possibly be any rehabilitation, and without rehabilitation reconciliation will undoubtedly lose its pragmatic effect" (2013a: 105).)

The poems written in New York called for a change of heart in the ruling elite but not for a different social structure. After the early 1970s, this social critique moved yet another stage further forward in *is Potret Pembangunan dalam Puisi* the name of a book or a poem? If it's a poem, the title and the translation should be be in quote marks. Also, there is no poem with the translated title on p109 or anywhere else in this anthology. Rendra's poems and activities increasingly protested against the political and economic policies promoted by the "New Order" regime (1965-1998), which he saw as no better than the old colonialism. The ruling elite were, in his opinion, committed to the politics of economic "Development" but not to improving the quality of human life. Rendra believed that these policies had, in fact, caused deep corruption among the elite, widespread poverty among the "little people", the degradation of the moral and spiritual values of daily life in general, and the constant domination of citizens by the surveillance of the police and the army. His "Angry Poem", written in 1979, for example, compared the luxury of the elite with the misery of the poor and insisted: "we say NO! and NO! to you". The poem described the poor as flowing water and the rich as cold heartless rocks, concluding that the rivers would eventually "wear away the rocks".

"Indonesia, May 1998" (written four days before Soeharto finally stepped down from the presidency on May 21) was a late assessment of "the dark days of kings", describing the New Order as "A mad age!/ A dark night of inhuman thought/ The pavilions of belief torn apart/ The law books shredded in the gutters./ Life's certainties staggering in the sewers". From the beginning of the era, Rendra's hopes for transformation had lain with the youth and in education, and he regularly participated in student meetings and demonstrations. In his later years, neither youthfulness nor education gave him complete confidence in the future, as the despondent ending of the poem "a Pile of Corn" showed. The title of his last volume, *Prayers for My Grandchildren*, comes, in part, from his response to a journalist who asked him: "What gives you the courage to protest against the government's development policies?" Rendra simply replied: "I do not protest and take a critical stance towards the government because I am courageous. On the contrary in fact. I do it because I am afraid of what might happen to my grandchildren in the future" (Rendra 2013b: xii-xiii).

A "*maskumambang*", the title of the second last poem in this collection, is a traditional Javanese verse form. The word itself means "gold floating on water", the gold caused by the rays of the setting sun perhaps but not real gold and therefore a cause for regret (Rendra 2013: 61-62). Rendra died in August 2009. He had passed illusion and entered the last phase of his life. He had decided that "It is Time" to accept the past, to live more simply, to seek reconciliation through the forms of non-violence (*ahimsa*), the acceptance of diverse viewpoints (*anekanta*) and non-covetousness (*aparigraha*). The sovereignty of human life, nature, society, of reason, were to be respected and lived out. All that remained to him, as he stated in his final poem, "God, I Love You", written while he was in hospital, was the desire "to go back to natural ways" and "to serve God better".

Rendra was considered by many to be Indonesia's most important poet during the second half of the twentieth century and until his death in 2009. He saw the world in deeply spiritual and personal ways, lived intensely, was profoundly socially committed, and embodied the Indonesian sense of what a true artist should be. He was faithful to his credo: "It is time to rise./ To bear witness./ To protect life". This book is his testimony to the sacredness of existence in all its complexity.

References

Fikar W Eda: "Rendra dan Aceh", in ed. Dwi Klik Santosa: *70 Tahun Rendra: Hadir dan mengalir!* Burungmerak, Bekasi Selatan 2005, pp. 112-117.

Jamal D Rahman: "Rendra", *33 Tokoh Sastra Indonesia Paling Berpengaruh*, KPG (Kepustakaan Populer Gramedia), Jakarta 2014, pp. 401-422.

Raffel, Burton: *The Development of Modern Indonesian Poetry*, State University of New York Press, Albany NY 1967.

Raffel, Burton: "A Personal Appreciation", in *Rendra: Ballads and Blues, Poems*, trans. Raffel, Burton; Harry Aveling and Derwent May, Oxford University Press, Kuala Lumpur 1974, pp. 258-265.

Rendra: *Blues untuk Bonnie*, Tjupumanik, Cirebon 1971.

Rendra: *Mastodon dan Burung Condor*, unpublished manuscript 1972, translated by Harry Aveling as "The Mastodon and the Condors," in ed. Cobina Gillitt: *The Lontar Anthology of Indonesian Drama*, volume 3, Lontar Foundation, Jakarta 2010, pp. 51-91.

Rendra: *Kisah Perjuangan Suku Naga*, unpublished manuscript 1975, translated by Max Lane as *The Struggle of the Naga Tribe*, University of Queensland Press, St Lucia 1979.

Rendra: *Potret Pembangunan dalam Puisi*, Pustaka Jaya, Jakarta 1993, translated by Harry Aveling (Swami Anand Haridas) as *State of Emergency*, Wild and Woolley, Sydney 1980.

Rendra: *Megatruh*, Kepel Press, Yogyakarta 2013a.

Rendra: *Doa untuk Anak Cucu*, ed. Edi Haryono, Bentang, Bandung 2013b.

Teeuw, A A: *Modern Indonesian Literature*, Nijhoff, The Hague 1967.

Trisno Sumardjo: "Penjair W.S. Rendra dalam 'Empat Kumpulan Sajak'," *Djaja*, 17 February 1962.

Testimony

Flowers Fall

Flowers fall
over the dead,
everything passes.

My darling.

Flowers fall
over your grave,
everything between us
comes to an end.

Let us promise
not to meet in heaven
no one makes love
in heaven.

Love belongs to this world
(where everything ends in death)
it follows us through our lives
and when our lives end
love ends too.

A few memories remain
they deceive us
and keep us from suicide.

Perhaps there is sorrow
a sign of respect
but it too will quickly pass.

My darling.

Falls, falls,
everything ends
life, love, the dew on the flowers—
we keep only what we can use.

Ballad of Kasan and Patima

When the lemon moon bursts open
Patima the old maid weeps.

She runs to the cemetery in the wasteland
unties her hair where the forest climbs upwards
coals and incense in her hands.

Patima! Patima!
her breasts and eyes are full of magic
a young man refused to marry her
disturbed by his fear of her spells.

Patima! Patima!
she beats on the door of a grave
by all the ghosts and demons
she shakes the sleep of the *kamboja* trees
wakes all the spirits from their broken graves
and with a voice as strange as the wind in the wilds
chants a prayer as her copper neck
stiffens her demon-filled face, while she gazes at the source of her
curse:

–Oh golden citrus moon, handsome young man,
push your face onto my sorrowing breast
wipe out the bitterness I bear
hot as lava, the vomit of the sun.

–Wretched Patima! Patima!
what is the cause of your sorrow, why do you want to torture him?

–Oh fairies of fire, demons of dark
heap up your curses, magic from the naked weapon wind
and drop them on Kasan's head!

–Should the lemon-trees and the flowering tamarinds lose their
leaves
because of Kasan, the man like a bull, like the night?
What sin has he committed, why do you curse him?

–The pain, oh the pain! a wound washed in vinegar
Kasan left me, resisted my will
carried away his flesh lips, so ripe and so firm,
that sucked so strongly the sweetness of my maidenhood.

And the wind says:
–May the dark twilight shelter him
as he rides away in the four-horse cart
with his wife and his children, to the west,
to a city in the hollow of the calm valley.
–He left me with my white hot passion
caressing a goat in its stall.

(Patima lies down in the light of the fire)

The wind, the grass and the falling leaves all gossip together:
–Kasan's wife's mouth tastes like coconut milk.
–And her eyes do not burn with magic.
–Her three children are white like ripe sweet-potatoes.
–Kasan, yes, Kasan! we know who he is!
At night the stars shine in his eyes
a slender man with hot blood
the faces of several maidens hidden in his heart.

Above me I saw
five girls yield themselves just like that
as the night brought forth flowers, moaning, singing
and Kasan roaring like a bull.

Patima waits with a curse.
–Loveless he knocked at the old maid's door.
–Her curse comes! Her curse comes!
–Patima chained him up for herself alone
once she felt that he cared for her
he bowed like a flower, she caressed his legs,
for herself alone! for herself alone!
that was what she wanted.
–Her curse comes! Her curse comes!
–And now he runs because his wife is fragrant like the jasmine
her mouth tastes like coconut milk.

The incense drifts and the *kamboja* trembles
Patima rises, her hands are like dry branches
the fire in her eyes licks at the face in the sky
and she sends her curse on Kasan's head. On Kasan!

Kasan driving his four-horse cart
is pulled from another direction in the dark
and hurled down the Southern Mountain, on the rocky soil,
his family cry out, the horses roar,
then the pitch-black night swallows them all.

–Her curse comes! Her curse comes!

At nights on the Southern Mountain a howl
thunders, rolling down the back of the mountains,
not the howl of the virile wind from the womb of the night:
but the roar of Kasan riding in his four-horse carriage
running with the curse hanging over him. Sour the vinegar—hot the
coals.

Ballad of the Death of Atmo Karpo

With hooves of steel the horse beats against the earth's belly
the treacherous moon rubs her body against the treetops
the fleeing bandit wraps his knees firmly around the creature
its mane stinks of sweat, his sword is drawn.

The villagers surround the forest
Atmo Karpo is coming home in a whirlwind
cursing the bitch moon and his wretched fate
flashing sparks of fire, an arrow in his left shoulder.

The men advance one by one, he draws their blood
the iron rider, his horse stamping its feet.

"Your souls are not your own, feeble minded fools!
Your spears are mere twigs. My death is far off.
Where is Joko Pandan? Let him step forward.
He is the only man I hate."

Arrows from four directions, enemies on all three sides.
Seven wounds in his body. Atmo Karpo still stands tall.

"Where is Joko Pandan?
He is the only man I hate."

His stomach slashed open, he is still a demon
he tugs at his horse, it rears its head.

"Where is Joko Pandan?
He is the only man I hate."

Joko Pandan appears, his horse announcing him,
The men step aside to let the black beast pass
his heart is filled with howling anger.

At their first step, both men are made of iron
at the third step, Atmo Karpo falls to the ground
his wounds are hot, his flesh open like red *angsana* petals.

Night is like a mask scored with wounds
the moon cheers and dances, drinking blood-red wine.

Joko Pandan rises, licking his sword.
He has killed his own father.

Guerrilla

Blue body
blue staring eyes
of the man dead in the street.

The wind hangs
spiced with tobacco bitterness
a dam of disaster and moaning.

Blue body
blue staring eyes
of the man dead in the street.

With seven bullet holes
he knocks at the gate of the sky
the early-morning sun burns
his hatred released.

A girl walking in the dawn redness
with vegetables on her back
sees him first.
She gives a sweet cry
sad like carrot-leaves.

Blue body
blue staring eyes
of the man dead in the street.

The villagers know him
the widow's son with wavy hair
they scoop water
and wash his body.

Blue body
blue staring eyes
of the man dead in the street.

Bravely he passed the Dutch guard
sheltered by the color of the night
and entered the town alone
to attend his mother's funeral.

Prisoner

On the bed of stone
his long body
a moonless row of hills
bent and subtle
his eyes denying the prison bars.

In the alleys
of his eyes
young men with red hands
attack Dutch soldiers.

Blood drips in his mouth
as he dreams
blood in a porcelain goblet.
He smiles
a coal in the belly of the mountain
(The hatred of the young men with red hands
carried on by their brothers).

Today sings
outside of him.
The bell
strikes six times
in its mother's belly.
Suddenly
he shuts his eyes.

The guard turns the key to his cell
And says:
"Hey rebel
Today is not for you!"

Dragged in front of the execution squad
he spits
not even telling them:
"Last night I tasted
the sweet honey of blood."

And he did not hear
the six rifles
fire together.

The Stubborn Child

The water in the river is cold.
Cold! Cold!
My sad flesh is cold
wrapped around my bones.

Hey, son!
Don't lean against a tree.
Come inside, son.
It is cold out there!

(Outside the wind dances in circles.
The boy rubs his back and bottom.
His father hit him and the child is angry.)

Although he is young
he puffs out his chest
and raises his tiny fist.
Oh! The young warrior
walking along a river of blood.

Hey, son!
The wind stirs the coals in your eyes.
Come in, son,
it is cold out there.

(Small leaves fall on his head
the boy stands in the road,
his hands on his hips.
A small stubborn child.)

Snot-nosed brat!
Why must a man be so stubborn
feeding on praise and conceit
warmed by his own dark blood?

Hey, son!
Your father's blood flows through your veins.
Smile and he will soften
He has no other hero but you.

And one smile will not betray you.
Come in, son!
It is cold outside!

(Under the black silk sky
with broken twigs at his feet
the boy puffs out his chest
hands on his hips
standing tall and stubborn.)

Woman, Waiting

People who wait,
Who wade through time,
Knowing no flowers in their heart
But only stone and air,

Are lonely morning and night,
Tortured by eternal boredom.

She sits on her wound,
Caressing it, and says:
"I'm old, and
I've been told

Just sit there–
And wait!"

Black River

Black river passing with a sigh
flowing from a nameless land.
Black river running through valleys.
Black river cutting through my breast.

It flows. Flows. Who knows from where?
A hermit secret, a secret grief.
Loneliness born of too much asking.
How it runs, that poisonous tongue!

Black Eyes

Two black eyes open out from a blue heart,
two black eyes that speak desire.
Desire isn't just for women, and
they both know, they've forgotten shyness.
Two black eyes set in fragrant flesh
that this silk does not hide.
Two black eyes: a dark dwelling
coffee in the afternoon and buried memories.

Black Rocks

Black river rocks, dreamless,
set groaning by uncaring children.
How stubborn, stiff, desiring nothing!
How hard, hard, smashing at motherless children!

An August wind: the moon smiles
But indifferent children remain indifferent.
Black stones are proud, cold.
Hidden bitterness frozen, covered with moss.

Scorched Earth

The heart always asks on scorched earth
could we have less? What's love worth?
The heart always asks on scorched ground
Where must we go, is there a roof for us?
The heart always asks on scorched earth
afraid of treachery
The heart always asks on scorched ground
Whose turn is it to die?

Violet Serenade

Then I heard a voice
from behind a bush
as the red moon lurched through the sky
and a breeze blew from the south.
Then I smelled a lovely fragrance,
the leaves rustled softly
as the insects buzzed
in the dark shadows.
Seven pairs of fairy eyes
watched from a tree.
Their faint, peculiar voices
and the distant perfume
made the night unreal.
Then I heard a voice
from behind a bush
making the grass tremble
and the river run dumb.
Two people
married by the moon.

Ostankino Church, Moscow

Its tall minaret
reaches up in vain.
Its door is a lonely mouth
snapped shut
swallowing fine dust.

Green Serenade

I spur my horse.
Spur him toward you.
The moon
greets me
and the clear evening
hangs from the branches.

Along a river of memories
which speaks of desire
and I can hear the soft moaning
of stones buried in the water.

I spur my horse.
spur him toward you
And I can almost see you
as you wait for me
braiding
your long hair.

Lullaby for a Bride

Clouds shake, trees sway,
angels fly between the bending trunks.
Far off a clear bell chimes.

Lovely solitude, sweet longing.
Narcotic longing, dust of desire.
Lie down, love, lay your face against my breast.

The sky is crimson, leaf-buds are crimson
my heart hangs in the crimson leaves
And the air is heavy with incantations.

Young dreams, a moon of memories,
The sadness of love, glittering, gleaming sadness.
Lie down, love, lay your dreams against my breast.

The earth goes to sleep.
Sadness melts.
I reach out and enfold you in my longing hands.

Silence and sleep, sleep and silence.
Silence without death, sleep without death.
Lie down, love, lay your sadness against my breast.

White Serenade

Her loneliness cages in her sorrow.
His quick glance tells her
he feels it too.
Outside someone strums a guitar
a lizard climbs the wall,
and yearning fills her:
like a dark shadow.
The clock on the wall
chimes.
He looks at it.
She lowers her eyes
her hair falls around her
like the night.
A hesitant girl
hiding her feelings
pretending.
She locks her lips.
And bows her head.
But the more she pretends
the warmer she grows.
Her sweet yearning
like an unpolished diamond,
like an untold secret.
The lizard chirps drowsily
and the silence in the room
quivers.
He touches her
and whispers
quietly.

A breeze bangs at the window.
His shoe bumps into a table-leg.
So:
in a trembling embrace
an urgent exchange of breath,
the key is found.

And then:
her first kiss.
And afterward:
they say everything.

Love Letter

I'm writing this letter
while the rain drizzles like a toy
drum played by tiny fairies
in some magic world.
And the wind sighs
puffs and sighs.
Hey, little sister Narti,
I love you!

I'm writing this letter
while the sky drips down
and two small wild ducks
are making love in the pond
like two naughty children
funny and nice
two flapping ducks
shaking their feathers.
Hey, little sister Narti,
I want you for my wife!

The rain's quick step
patters along the ground.
Like gleaming, heavy metal
love walks steadily
forward
never turning back.

Twelve angels
have descended
in the drizzling rain.
In the window glass
they stare and wash their hair
to prepare for the celebrations.
Hey, little sister Narti
in my elegant bridegroom clothes
covered with flowers and wearing a sacred sword
I ache to lead you to the altar
and marry you.

I asked for you.
You knew long ago:
I am no worse
and no better
than all the others…
I'm a poet of small, ordinary things,
I began with words,
and words begin
with life, thought, and feeling.

The sweet strong pleasure of life
is like a million tiny needles
stabbing through the sky:
a purse of gold and a sharp blessing.
Then the rain pours down.
Love and the wind
sigh helplessly in the drizzle.
The sweet strong pleasure of my love
is like a thousand invisible hands
spreading a thousand nets
to catch your heart
as it steadily smiles at me.

You're a mermaid princess
my captive.
A mermaid princess
your voice is as gentle
as a sea breeze,
sighing for me!
The wind sighs
and sighs
in a clear sweet lament.
You're a mermaid princess
turning softly
blinking your beautiful eyes
in my net.
Oh mermaid princess,
I caught you,
I asked for you.

I'm writing this letter
as the rain drips
because the sky
is a sweet, spoiled child
crying for her toys.
Two mischievous little boys
are having fun in the ditch
and the jealous sky is watching them.
Hey, little sister Narti,
I want you
to be the mother of my children!

Episode

We were sitting
on a bench in front of her house.
The rose-apple tree
was heavy with fruit
and we watched it, happy.
The passing wind played
with the falling leaves.
Then she asked, suddenly:
"Why is your shirt-button
open?"
I only laughed.
So she gently pinned it
shut.
And as she did
I picked a fallen petal
from her hair.

Invitation

With our sincere compliments
We hope that Mr/Mrs/Miss
will attend our wedding ceremony...

Bread rises
yeast and flour joined.
Trees sprout and bear fruit
seeds scatter, multiply,
across the face of the earth.

Place:
St Joseph's Church, Bintaran, Yogyakarta

God's ancient house,
Our Father's peaceful lap.
Everything
Must begin somewhere.
Tall trees
Grow from this sacred soil.

Time:
Tuesday, 31 March 1959,
at 10 am, Javanese time...

A new day begins
continuing the circle
that turns without end.
Since the very first light
this world has been shaped
by God's Almighty Hands.

And with our sincere compliments
we say thank you
both before and after the ceremony.

The Moon's Bed, the Bride's Bed

The moon's bed, the bride's bed
an azure blue sky
held up by the hands of our ancestors.
A cricket flutters about
shrilling a love song to the net.

The moon's bed, the bride's bed
a Chinese junk with a thousand sails
crossing the sea of sleep;
Stars fall one by one
yawning with sweet visions.

The moon's bed, the bride's bed
a kingdom of ghosts and spirits
drunk on the odor of incense.
Dreams scatter one by one,
to be tested by time.

The moon's bed, the bride's bed
the harsh earth of reality
colored by pleasure and hope.
Dry soil toiled over
Seeded, made fertile.

The moon's bed, the bride's bed:
An ivory bed.
A porcelain bed.
An alabaster bed.

A stone bed.
A wind-blown bed.
Paved with asphalt.
Newly-weds swallowed up by life,
Eyes to the future, hand in hand.

The Moscow River

On Sunday
Valya laughs
and her blond hair
spreads out.

We sail along
in a small red boat
passing the time.

The banks
are lined with trees
one for each of our sins.
All the leaves
are changing color.
It's autumn now.

We glide over
the green water
followed by vague shadows.
We float under the arc of a bridge
like an arc into nothingness.
It's autumn now.

Valya laughs
her breasts shake
inside her sweater.
It's autumn, now.

Aichun Hotel, Canton

In the peaceful afternoon
I open the wide window
for a breath of outdoor air.
The friendly sky
and the rows of *lichee* branches
are reflected
on the window pane.
The bells ring
twelve times.
And an electric fan spins.
Everything's calm, everything's at peace.

Looking down
I see people lazy in the heat
along the brick road.
And further off
I see the Pearl River,
weariest of them all
Weary but at peace.

The Chinese silk curtain is full of flowers
and makes this room lovely.
I dress, carefully,
in front of the big dresser mirror
carved with dragons,
I am alone, peaceful.

Now I feel that peace
having wrestled with myself last night
and soothed longing with comprehension.
Of course
I still remember
home
but patiently now.
Not writing poems
not sticking to my books
I only want to relish this aloneness.
And as I blow smoke rings
I am content with this
quite adequate vacation.

A Saint

1

He is a saint.
He lies beside the road
and waits for death.
A saint is a man who sins
and always rises again.
A saint is a man who beats his breast
and cries:
"Father, I am a sinful child!"
He is a saint
He is a sinner.
He has traveled far–
From hunger to crime.
From prison to despair.
From sin to his God.
Someone says:
"He's an unlucky sort
driven to do things
through no fault of his own, despicable things.
And he was fair to everyone else
but always forgot about himself."
And now he awaits death
wounds all over his body.
His breath comes bit by bit
and he seems to see God in front of him.
People pity him
as they come.

Some say:
"I gave him that wound."
"Yes, I cracked him on the head."
"Ah, we've all wounded
his mouth, his chest, his neck,
his belly, and his soul."
But he only smiles
gasping for breath and filling us with sorrow.

2

The crowd sobs, weeping,
talking:
"How strange he was, always sacrificing himself."
"He didn't like to see old people carrying things
and always helped them."
"He was like dice
in a tin can
shaken vigorously.
The world is that whirling container."
"When he fell he always rose again.
He wept easily but he was determined.
He worried, but he knew what he believed.
He was a meddler."
"And we know he was good."
"Yes, yes, a good man
with eyes like a cow about to be slaughtered."
"We were always together on the road.
We both shook with hunger.
And he smiled at me.
Ah! The way he smiled
as if he knew hell and human misery.

Yes, he knew
how to respond
when sorrow came calling."
He stretched out his body
still bleeding from its wounds.
In the end
he met death,
with both arms outstretched.

3

The crowd weeps and sobs
people bow their head.
Then a woman passes by and asks:
"Who was he?
What was his name?"
A man answers:
"A saint has died
a holy man has gone to his reward."
"But wasn't he the young fellow
who broke into a restaurant
and was beaten by the woman who owned it
who wept, a weakling?
And didn't other people come
and beat him too?
I saw three small children
waiting outside, trembling,
and they wept when they saw what happened to him.
Where are they now?
And what was his name?"
"A stupid man from a drought stricken village
come here to die.
We never knew his name.

A good man who died without a name.
He tried to reject evil.
But his life was chosen for him.
He cried with confusion
not because people hit him.
He was a saint.
He wept for holiness."
"Yes, yes, he was a saint.
He was crucified.
The sins of the world crucified him!
And as for his children
No one knows where they have gone.
Ah!
Will they be crucified too
like their father?"

Prayer of the Hungry

Hunger is
a cunning black crow.
Millions of crows
like a black cloud.
O God!
Crows are terrifying.
And hunger is a black crow.
Continually terrifying.
Hunger is rebellion.
It is the mysterious force
moving the murderer's knife
in the hands of the poor.
Hunger is coral
beneath the sleeping face of the sea.
It is tears of deceit.
It is the betrayal of honor.
A strong young man weeping
to see his hands
lay down honor
because of hunger.
Hunger is a devil.
Hunger is a devil offering dictatorship
O God!
Hunger is black hands
putting handfuls of alum
into the stomachs of the poor.
O God!
We kneel.

Our eyes are Your eyes.
This is your mouth.
This is your heart.
And this is your stomach.
Your stomach is hungry, O God.
Your stomach chews alum
and broken glass.

O God!
How nice it would be
to have a plate of rice
a bowl of soup and a cup of coffee.
O God!
Hunger is a crow.
Millions of black crows
like a black cloud
blotting out my view
of Your heaven.

Rose Psalm

Let us praise the Name of God.
Let us praise Him with roses.
Let us praise the king of kings.
Let us praise God, sweet,
beautiful and merciful.
God is the wounded soldier.
God walks along the dirty roads
like a wise old man
in a torn clothing
caressing the heads of hungry children.
God is a middle-aged man coughing
wisely and calmly
stroking the head of a prostitute.
God lives in the dark alleys
with thieves, bandits
and murderers.
God is the friend in the room with adulterers.
King of all kings
worms for geese and pigs to eat.
God's sweet face is a dusty gambling table
pelted with cards.
Now I see God as
a worn-out old man
sleeping in the gutter
coughing in the cold
his hand pressing against his hungry belly.

God is attacked by hunger, cold and flu
and cries at the edge of the road.
He is our best friend!
He is the friend of all of us: enemies of the police.
bandits, murderers, gamblers,
prostitutes, the unemployed and beggars.
Let us come to Him—
Let us help our kind old friend.

The World's First Face

In the pale moonlight
he carries his bride
up that hill.
Both of them naked.
Bringing nothing but themselves.

In the beginning
the world is bare
empty, free of lies.
Darkness confronted by silence.

And that silence sinks
into the depths of time.
Next comes light
the existence of creatures
people and animals.
In the beginning
everything is bare
empty and open.

The young bride and groom
have followed a long path.
Through dawn lit by their imaginations
the skies filled with hope
rivers lined with comfort
they enter the day's furnace
dripping with sweat.

And as they stand on a barren coral reef.
evening comes again
bringing dreams
and a bed of rest
lined with gleaming coral necklaces.
They raise their heads to see
thousands of stars in the sky.
As many as their descendants.
Thousands and thousands.
Never-ending.

In the pale moonlight
he carries his bride
up that hill
both of them naked
the world's first face.

Knife in the Road

There's a knife lying in the road
and the sun quivers across it.
There's a knife lying in the road
and dried blood on its blade.
No one knows
the final, bitter thirst
it fed,
or where.
A rigid body,
forgotten somewhere.
One day a wound bled
and no one mourned.
A black death
with no headstone.
And a blue corpse
soon forgotten.
No purifying water.
No broken fruits
to cleanse his wrinkled, dusty skin.
Cursed clouds
with death in their pockets
and evil grins
steal his face
There's a knife lying in the road
and the sun quivers across it.

Hotel International, Pyongyang

Late at night
my restless hands open the balcony door
and I wrestle with my loneliness.
An unfriendly autumn night
keeps the streets empty.
The trees stand like bent old women.
Except for the wind nothing moves.
In such solitude one examines oneself
confronts oneself
nakedly.
The Pyongyang wind rumples my hair
asking:
"Boy with the tousled hair
whose son are you?"
Then I see my tense face,
my nervousness, my restless heart.
I try to be friendly, greet myself:
"Hello! Is anyone there?"
The late night trembles and turns grey.
Loneliness confronts me like a mirror.
"Hey, young fellow!
You are not an old man yet!"
And then I'm embarrassed
though I don't have to be
and I know it.

Morning Psalm

The words of my psalm
ascend to heaven
in the kitchen smoke
as my wife boils milk
on the stove–
Your first blessing to mankind.
The words of my psalm
run from valley to valley
and at the edge of the horizon
marry the silence
which has long awaited them.
Buffalo enter the river
stir up the pure water
denying twilight
and the final judgment.
And
in the fresh air
perfume scatters
from the robe of an angel.
You set Your beautiful body down
in the high mountains
from below it seems
like a cloud bathed in light.
Ducks lay eggs
at the touch of Your hand.

Fish leap in the water
and the rice stalks wave
greeting You.
The pine trees in the mountains
tickle Your feet
mischievously.
So You rise
to go to another sky
laughing and scattering beauty
walking, rising up with the sun.
And the sun climbs
and climbs and climbs,
drying the shirt and trousers
my wife washed.

Evening Prayer

God in heaven.
From this narrow bamboo house
on this cold evening
my fragile hands
reach out towards heaven.
I will sleep in Your eyes
which are filled with rainbows
and valleys like soft velvet mattresses.
When the wind brushes
Your curly long hair
I will kneel at the threshold of Your ears
and say my prayers.
Prayers are the dreams
and hopes of mankind.
I will whisper my dreams.
Does that make You laugh?
My small child
will climb up Your robe
and sleep in Your pocket.
With the moon over Your shoulder
my wife will sail in Your blood.
When You say goodnight
multicolored paper flowers
scatter from Your mouth.
And You prepare a blue balloon
for my son.
The stars clap their hands
and the insects laugh
in amazement:

You are the Incomparable Magician.
Then You lift Your phosphorescent hands
shining, high, shining.
And that means: sleep well
see you tomorrow
I'll have other magic tricks then.

An Angry World

After two world wars
the chatter of guns and munitions in the air,
how does the world look now?
After so many speeches and conferences
the establishment of fine institutions
merely to quarrel
through a thousand slogans
and stab each other in the back,
how does the world breathe now?

Here in this part of the earth
there are wounded faces
in the dark night of the spirit.
We do not need a map
to show where our people are.
This is an angry world.
Full of bright vicious eyes,
cruel hopeless faces,
and trembling hands
grasping at empty life.
In which
homes, men and rubbish
are all one.
Full of impotent bitterness.

World wars and rebellion
did not change our weary earth.
Murder after murder
hatred after hatred
gave birth to nothing
but sin, doubt,
and disbelief.

Gave birth to nothing
except the sacrifice of the powerless.
The continually questioning faces!
Driven into a world
of confusion and lies
they are always alone.
They grow from sin. They give birth to sin.

Our world is always wounded.
The poor walk with their hunger.
They are like thin dead sticks.
They regret their birth
but refuse to die.
They are sterile. They produce nothing.
They cling to the earth–
for that is their mother.
The others are their enemies.

In our tattered world
the poor beat out their bloody lives
suffering sin
unconsciously. Unwillingly.
God stands amongst them
He is wounded with them.
And the world rejects Him.

God cries with them.
But they do not hear Him.
God is sad and suffering
buffeted by angry feet.
Buffeted by bitterness
and restless fear.

Father!
Avoiding death
is their main problem
not welfare or sin.
How can they understand the voice of heaven
if they have never heard the voice of life?

Father!
While the world understands only guns and deceit
stretch out Your loving hands
Your loving wounded heart.
Your wounds! Father, Your wounds!
Only through wounds
can the world understand love.

God cries and understands.
God continually cries and understands.
He is always stabbed. Always betrayed.

A Soldier's Prayer Before Battle

My God
Your face is reflected in the burning city
and Your words are scratched
across thousands of shallow graves.

Children weep for their fathers.
The land longs for its men.
It is not seed scattered across the fertile earth
but corpses and the faces of the dead
who have died for nothing.

When the sun sets
the color of sin will be perfect
and weapons will speak again.
Then, my God,
allow me to kill
allow me to use my bayonet.

Night and my face
will be the same color.
Sin and my breath
will share the same air.
There is no other choice
but to realize this
and to regret it.

What can my obedient lips say?
I see Your weary hands
embracing a world that betrays You.
My God,
I hold my rifle tightly.
Allow me to kill.
Allow me to use my bayonet.

An Old Man's Poem for His Wife

I am writing this poem
to comfort you.
As I remember your rheumatism,
I remember our shining youth.
And our future
which is almost finished,
almost willingly fulfilled.

We are not alone,
or unaware of our fate.
It is the law of life.
Our joys and sorrows are nothing special,
everyone experiences them.

Life is not meant for complaining.
Life is for living,
for working the land,
exploring the secrets of the sea and the sky,
for creating and for measuring the world.
We bear our burdens,
what must be done must be done.
Not to earn heaven or escape hell.
But out of respect for human dignity.

We are not dust,
even though we are frail, old and gray.
We are individuals
who respect themselves.
Look back
to the past no one can erase.

See how our years are filled with color.
Ninety years caressed by our breath,
Ninety years of successful struggle,
through times of confusion.
And remember too
how we always smiled
as we faced heaven and earth, and our fate.

We smiled, we were not acting,
not wearing masks
not doing what others thought we should.
We believed in God, humanity,
fate, and in life itself.

Look! Ninety years full of color!
Remember how we refused to live in a coma.
We are shaky and bent over
because age is more powerful than we are
not because we have been defeated.

I am writing this poem
to comfort you.
As you remember your rheumatism
remember that we have faced the challenges
of a hundred gods.

I Call Your Name

As I cross the loneliness
I call your name, my wife.
Why can't you hear me?

The night moans
embracing my weary spirit
troubled
by rebellion towards home
rebellion towards meaningless custom
and is finally taunted by the heavens.

I search for the light of your eyes.
I want to remember the fragrance of your body
which I can no longer recall.
It is futile.
There is nothing I can hold.
My loneliness is perfect.

The wind of rebellion
attacks land and sky.
Twelve jackals
appear from my past
and tear at my wretched heart.

Over and over I call your name.
Where are you, my wife?
Have you too become part of my past?
I call your name.

I call your name
because you are a house in the valley.
And God?
God is the inscrutable artist
who always
only cares about big things.

A thousand fingers from my past
point accusingly at me.
No.
I cannot go back.

As I continue to call your name
the pure anger of my rebellion
rises bravely this night
and scatters itself into the heavens
which like a naked girl
open themselves to me.
Full. And virginal.

The silence that follows
is like a large cold lake
and I am frozen at its edge.
My face. Look at my face.
Reflected in the silence.
Wounded and bleeding
clawed by my past.

For MG

You came into my life
at a critical time.
I came into your life
when you were like
a wild horse
in need of a plain.
(And had even forgotten the name of your in-laws).
Why question the meaning of our embrace?
You moaned when I molded your breast with my hand.

Misery slept with lust
to produce children and multiply.
With the bed wet from your sweat
I said:
you are like an eel.
which was to say:
though I may know each curve of your body
your soul still slips free from my grasp.

I tore you from
your emptiness
from alcoholic New York
neon light fantasies
and your slurred questions
riding up and down the elevator.
I dragged you off
to plunge you into my predicament
my revulsion towards hunger
my philosophy of rebellion
and doubt.

My God, your blond hair
was so strange
it gave me new passion.

I was a scoundrel
yet you received me.
Yielded to me.
Like a ship you carried me
to chart the anxious air
of your quick breath
and rippling body.

Life came alive and stirred.
Time trembled in the trembling space.
When your lips dried and paled
and your fingernails pressed into my shoulders
I squeezed my eyes shut.

My life and your life
were not changed.
Each keeping its own sphere.
Each keeping its own riddles
to torment us time and again.

Blues for Bonnie

Boston is withered and faded
from blustering winds, awful weather,
and a late night's bad luck.
In the cafe
an old black man
plays his guitar and sings.
There is barely an audience.
Only seven couples
cheating and loving in the dark
billowing gray clouds of cigarette smoke,
like sputtering furnaces.

He sings.
His voice is deep.
He marries song and words
To give birth to a hundred meanings.
Georgia. Far away Georgia.
Where his people's shacks stand
With leaky roofs.
Earthworms and malnutrition.
Far away Georgia he calls it in his song.

People stop talking
There is no sound.
Save that of the wind shaking the windowpanes.
Georgia.

With his eyes clamped shut
the man hails silence.
And silence replies
with a swift blow
to his gut.

In his pain
he behaves like a gorilla.
An old and stooped gorilla
roaring.
His fierce fingers claw the guitar
as he scratches the itch in his soul.

Georgia.
No new customers arrive.
The air outside is bitter.
The wind blusters even more.
And a cold bed awaits him
at the hotel.
The cafe's proprietor scowls
Because of tonight's losses.
The black man looks up.
Straining the cords in his neck.
His dry red eyes
stare at heaven.
And heaven
throws down a net
to snare his body.

Like a black fish
he struggles in the net.
Thrashing about
in vain.

Angry
ashamed
and futile.

The wind beats across Boston Commons.
Whistles in the church towers.
And tears the night to shreds.
The black man stamps his foot.
Sings his oaths and curses.
His white teeth shine
in a tight grin of revenge.
His face is dirty, wet and old
like a moss-covered stone.

Time, like a flood
overwhelms his weary soul.
And in the middle of it all
he feels a tremendous jerk
in his leg.
Surprised
and near incredulous
he feels
rheumatism
rip through his limb.

Like a good showman
he hides his surprise.
Slowly stops.
Slowly sits on his stool.
A cracked vase on a stand
in a secondhand store.
And after drawing a deep breath
he begins to sing once more.

Georgia.
Far away Georgia he calls it in his song.
His wife's still there
Devoted but suffering.
Black kids play in the ditches
not comfortable in school.
The old ones are drunks and braggarts
and forever in debt.
On Sunday mornings
they go to the black church.
Where they sing
spellbound by the hope of the Second Coming
and their lack of power on earth.

Georgia.
Mud sticks to shoes.
Shacks without windows.
Suffering and the world,
each as old as the other.
And heaven and hell
time-worn, too.
But Georgia?
Dear God.
Even after running so far,
Georgia is still on his heels.

Rick from Corona

(In the Queens Plaza
subway station
there was written on the wall:
"Rick from Corona was here.
Where were you, Betsy?")

Yeah....
Rick from Corona was here.
Where were you, Betsy?

—I'm Betsy
Here I am.
Betsy Wong from Jamaica.
My great-grandfather came from Hong Kong.
My husband's an elevator operator
Pedro Gonzales from Puerto Rico
a liar and drunk.
If you want to get together, give me a ring.
Mornings I work at a bakery
Tuesday and Thursday nights
I belong to Mickey Ragolsky
this old Polish guy
who pays the rent on my room.
Try calling on Wednesday.
Don't worry about my husband.
He'll pretend not to know.
Oh, yeah, before I forget:
it'll cost ya twenty bucks.

My Betsy is pure and white
soft and smooth like a rubber sponge.
Her hair is long and thick
like a skein of gold yarn.
And her legs are perfect.
Long and smooth
like a salmon.

(Rick from Corona
in the bowels of New York
looks right and left
and drinks his orange soda).

Betsy.
Where are you, Betsy?

—Here, Betsy Hudson here.
I love nature
but hate farming.
I believe in all sorts of fairy tales.
I believe in Atlantis.
And that life on the moon
must be better than life on earth.
But I don't believe in politics.
My name is Betsy.
Really.
But there's no way we can meet.
Days I work as an accountant.
Nights I write in my diary.
And besides, taking care of myself
my hair and nails
all that uses up time too.

My name is Betsy.
I'm something to look at.
I like to stand naked in front of the mirror.
I hate men.

(In his British sports car
and ink-black sunglasses
Rick from Corona
cruises New York.
He is stopped by the cops
for a traffic violation
in the middle of a daydream.)

Betsy shines like the lights of Broadway.
Betsy is beautiful when she flies.
Her perfume puts New York to sleep.
And always, after that
she covers me
with a cotton blanket
that she made herself.
Betsy, where are you, Betsy?

—Here I am, stupid!
You never listen to me, Ricky!
You're always picking fights,
You never put your shoes on the rack.
You always wear those loud ties.
How many times have I told you
not to snore when you sleep.
It's barbaric.
And, Ricky!
You gotta stop slurping your soup!

(New York spreads its legs.
Hard and arrogant.
Cement and steel.
Cold and rigid.
In the middle of the bright lights
comes the sound of restless music
which of course
means nothing.)

Rick from Corona was here.
Yeah, yeah.
Betsy, where were you?

–Ricky, honey, I'm here.
Yeah, yeah.

+You're black.
You're not Betsy.
You're a black tiger from Harlem.

–Squeeze my ass.
Feel how soft and full it is.
My name's Betsy. Yeah, yeah.

+My girl always takes the time
to answer my stupid uncertain questions.

–I'm Betsy because I'm black.
Because I'm black
I'm in your hands.
I'm Betsy. Yeah.
I decided my name is Betsy.

+Drugs, drugs.
I long for mystical experience
I want to paint your naked body
while smoking marijuana.

–Ricky, honey, I'll sing you a lullaby
And like a baby you can adore my tits.

+From Queens. From Brooklyn. And from Manhattan–

–Ricky, honey, my loving eagle.

+Because of the combo rhythm, because of the saxophone swing–

–Shut your eyes.
And play me
like a banjo.

(In Harlem, Manhattan, New York
where people live in huddled masses
the air smells of rubbish and piss
in summer when it's ninety-five
the blacks watusi in the street
and when it climbs to a hundred and two
they begin to roll).

Hello. Hello.
This is Rick from Corona.
Betsy's here too–
Hello, Doctor.
We need some shots right away.
Cause we got a royal dose.

A Worldly Song

As the moon sleeps on an old mattress
I caress a maiden in the mango grove.
Her heart is wild and fiery
trampling hunger and thirst underfoot.
In our misery we reach out.
The passion of our rebellion
roars in the dark and the shadows.
And her fierce laughter
makes my heart glad.

In the shadows of the trees
her body shines
like a golden deer.
Her unfinished breasts
are like half ripe fruits.
The sweet smell of her body
is like the smell of grass.
I embrace her
as I embrace life and death
And her fast breathing
whispers in my ears.
She is amazed
at the rainbow
beneath her hooded lids.

Our ancient ancestors
appear from the centre of the dark
coming nearer
in their ragged clothing
and squat
watching us.

Testimony, 1967

The world we are building is a world of steel,
glass and wind swept mines.
Tomorrow's world is no longer virginal,
but ravaged and open to all
like some unrestrained slut.
The dreams we chase are dreams of shining platinum.
The world we walk is a world of poverty.
The situation that imprisons us is the gaping jaw of a jackal.

Our fate flies like a cloud
opposing and mocking us,
becoming mist in the sleep of night
and sun in the work we do each day.
We will die in the riddle of our fate
with arrogant and clenched hands.
Hands that rebel and labor.
Hands that tear at the sacred envelope
and unfold the holy letter
written in difficult characters we cannot read.

Twilight View

The wet twilight soothes the burning forest.
Vampire bats descend from the dark grey sky.
Smell of munitions in the air. Smell of corpses.
Smell of horseshit.
A pack of wild dogs
eat hundreds and thousands of human bodies
the dead and the half dead.
And among the scorched trees of the forest
puddles of blood form a lake.
Wide and calm. A deep dark red.
Twenty angels come down from heaven
to purify those in their death throes
but on earth they are ambushed by the vampire bats
and raped.
A vital breeze travels gently on
moving the ringlet curls of the corpses
making circles on the lake of blood
and strengthening the lust of the angels and bats.
Yes, my brothers,
I know this is a view that satisfies you
for you have worked so intently to create it.

Prostitutes of Jakarta, Unite!

The prostitutes of Jakarta
the greatest and the least
have been crushed
hunted.
They are frightened
lost
offended and embarrassed.

Regret as you may.
But don't despair.
Or allow yourselves to be sacrificed.

Prostitutes of Jakarta.
Arise now.
Comb your hair.
Having sorrowed
it is your turn
not just to defend yourselves
but to attack.
So:
Regret as you may
but do not allow yourselves to be sacrificed.

Sarinah!
Tell them
how you were called to the ministerial suite
and how he spoke long and deeply to you
about the national struggle
then suddenly—without even finishing what he was saying
calling you the inspiration of the revolution
undid your bra.

And you, Dasima.
Tell the people
how all the leaders of the revolution
embraced you in turn
speaking of the prosperity of the masses
and the flame of revolution
while their trousers were wet
and their bodies
sprawled beside you.
Their bolts too rapidly shot.

The politicians and senior civil servants
are a tight bunch of rogues.
Their congresses and conferences
couldn't run without you.
You who can never say "no"
because of the terror of hunger
the yoke of poverty
and your long futile search for work.
School diplomas were useless.
The section heads
would only open the door of opportunity
if you opened your legs.
And outside government
were only run down businesses
with no vacancies–
The leader's revolution
was a revolution for gods.
They fought for heaven
and not for this earth.
A revolution by gods
has never produced
more jobs
for the ordinary people.

You are a part of the proletariat
they have created.
So:
Regret as you may
But don't despair
or allow yourselves to be sacrificed.

Prostitutes of Jakarta.
Stop being ashamed.
When I read in the papers
how those clowns persecute you
accuse you of being the source of all the nation's disasters
I am enraged.
You are my friends.
I can't have this.
God.
What clownmouths
What foulmouths
They have even politicized sex.

My sisters.
It is harder to ban you
than a political party.
They must give you work.
They must return your standing.
They too must bear the weight of their mistakes.

My sisters. Unite.
Take up sticks.
Wave your bras on the ends of them.
Carry them around the town in procession
waving them like flags they have disgraced.
Now it is your turn to make demands.

Tell them:
That recommending the persecution of prostitutes
without also recommending
marrying them too
is nonsense.

Prostitutes of Jakarta.
My sisters.
Do not tremble before men.
You can easily strip the fakes.
Double your prices
and let them flounder.
Strike for a month
confuse them
and soon they will be committing adultery
with their brothers' wives.

A Pickpocket's Advice to His Mistress

Sitti,
Now that I understand your position a little better
I shall deceive you no longer
with talk of marrying you
and leaving your man.

(The bats fly chasing each other
a sign evening is drawing near.
I sing in the bathroom
as I wash my elegant body.
Oh, my sweetheart, my lover
I shall wait for you on the corner
wearing my lace-blouse
and new skirt.)

Your fate is a reasonable one.
From servant to mistress of an office-head.
What more could you want?
Marrying me would only spoil your chances.
They days to come will obviously be difficult enough.
As a pickpocket my fate is chancy.
Which is not exactly news.
But I am not the right sort of father
for the baby you bear in your womb.

(The bats fly chasing each other
a sign evening is drawing near.
The sun vomits painfully into the sea
stifling the people of Jakarta.

Oh, the wind.
Oh, my lover.
My nerves tremble
waiting for your tongue
to lick my body.)

I have never doubted your love for me
But love is secondary.
Looking after yourself comes first.
Our hearts must be prepared
to struggle for your child's future.
Start cheating your man right away.
Siphon off what he owns.
To make your own life easier.
Your man is a normal sort of senior civil servant
he enjoys being bribed and corrupting others.
Cheat him in return
that's how it's done.
Thieves cheat thieves, that's usual.
Besides
among thieves honor is like lipstick.
Remember cunning above all.
Second courage.
And third perseverance.
Fourth resoluteness, even in telling lies.
This is how thieves live.
Don't worry then.
The little people can't stay beaten forever.

(The bats fly chasing each other
a sign evening is drawing near.
I must pass you by today
for he has suddenly come.

Tonight
the foolish clown will play the acrobat
in my bed.)

Always strive to improve your position.
Strive to meet a minister
and to be his mistress.
Even though as the mistress of a minister
you still retain your former lover.
If he rejects your liaisons
as he keeps liaisons with you and his wife
it means he doesn't understand himself.
Embrace him.
Don't let your lack of education scare you
as long as you are vigorous and your breasts are firm.
That always attracts a minister.
Your idle chatter will be of no account
as long as you are spirited, assured and quite confident.
The very model of a minister in fact.

(The bats fly chasing each other
a sign evening is drawing near.
My thoughts fly back to that moment
when, busy watching the parade
you pinched my behind
thar's how we met
at least, after I stepped on your foot.
And now, each evening
like an over-ripe banana
I wait for your hand
to open me up.)

Finally, what I hope for your child.
Guard him day and night.
It's very likely he'll be a boy.
Teach him to fight
to have no qualms about hitting from behind.
Don't let him judge a man by his character.
There are only two possibilities, friend or foe.
Friends may be useful for a while.
An enemy is always evil.
And must be hit until he's crushed.
This is the essence of the art of self-survival.
Teach him to seek a high position.
God forbid he be a teacher or a professor.
That's a miserable thing, no money
If he can, let him be a policeman or a soldier
so that he doesn't have to buy rice
but gets it from the state.
With a nice uniform
legally or not
his rights must always come first.
When he wheedles as easily as you do
and his face is as smooth as mine–well!
This is the perfect combination.
Meaning that he has a talent for politics.
Who knows, maybe a member of parliament.
Or even a minister.
At least he will be a success in Jakarta.

(The bats fly chasing each other
a sign evening is coming on.
Buses light their lamps.
Women put on lipstick.
Tell me my darling
where we shall meet next time.)

Swan Song

The owner of the brothel said to her:
"You have been down for two weeks now.
You are getting sicker.
You are not bringing in any money.
In fact you owe me money.
I do not like losing money.
I can carry you no longer.
Today you must leave."

(The angel who guards paradise
whose face is bright and malicious
whose sword burns
points accusingly at me.
My blood freezes.
Maria Zaitun is my name.
An unfortunate whore.
Not pretty enough and too old.)

Twelve o'clock in the afternoon.
The sun high in the sky.
No wind. No clouds.
Maria Zaitun leaves the brothel.
No suitcase.
No possessions.
Her friends look away.
She sways as she walks.
Body fevered.
Syphilis burning her.

Ulcers on her crotch
neck, armpits, breasts.
Her eyes are red.
Her lips dry.
Her gums bleed.
Her heart troubles her again

She goes to the doctor's.
Where many are waiting before her.
And sits among them.
Suddenly they move aside, holding their nostrils.
She swears angrily
but the nurse quickly grabs her by the arm.
She takes her turn before them
and no one complains.

"Maria Zaitun
you owe me quite a bit of money," says the doctor.
"Yes," she replies.
"How much do you have?"
"None."
The doctor shakes his head and orders her to undress.
It hurts as she undoes her blouse
and the cloth sticks to an ulcer under her armpit.
"That's enough," says the doctor.
Not even examining her.
Then he whispers to the nurse:
"Give her an injection of vitamin C."
Startled the nurse whispers back:
"Vitamin C?
Doctor, wouldn't she be better off with penicillin?"
"Why?

She cannot pay.
And she is nearly dead.
Why give her expensive medicines
imported from overseas?"
(The angel who guards paradise
whose face is spiteful and malicious
whose sword burns
points accusingly at me.
I tremble with fear.
I can feel nothing. Think nothing
Maria Zaitun is my name.
An unfortunate and frightened whore.)

One o'clock in the afternoon.
The sun still at its peak.
Maria Zaitun walks without shoes.
And the cheap asphalt
melts beneath her feet.
She walks towards the church.
The door is locked.
Because they are afraid of thieves.
She goes to the presbytery and pushes the bell.
The sexton comes out and says:
"What do you want?
Father is still having lunch.
And this is not his hour for seeing people."
"I'm sorry. I'm sick. This is urgent."
The sexton examines her dirty foul body.
Then says:
"As long as you stay outside you can wait.
I'll ask Father if he will see you."
Then the sexton leaves closing the door.
She waits dazed by the sun.

An hour later the priest comes.
After picking the remains of the meal from his teeth
he lights a cigar, then asks:
"What do you want?"
His mouth smells of wine.
His slippers are made of crocodile skin.
Maria Zaitun replies:
"I want to confess my sins."
"But this isn't the confessional hour.
This is my time for prayer."
"I want to die."
"Are you sick?"
"Yes. I have VD."
On hearing this, the priest takes two steps back.
He scowls.
Finally a little confused he speaks again:
"Are you–er–a lady of the night?"
"I'm a prostitute. Yes."
"By St Peter! But you're a Catholic!"
"Yes."
"By St Peter!"
There is no sound for three moments.
The sun continues to burn.
Then the priest speaks again:
"Were you led into sin?"
"Not led. But I have sinned greatly."
"You were deceived by the devil."
"No. I was forced by poverty.
And my failure to find a job."
"By St Peter!"
"By St Peter! Father, listen to me.
I don't need to know why I sinned.
I realize my life has been a failure.

My soul is confused.
And I want to die.
But I am terribly afraid.
I need God or whatever
to be my friend."
The face of the priest becomes deep red.
He points at Maria Zaitun.
"You are some sort of wild tiger.
Maybe you are mad.
But you are not going to die.
You don't need a priest.
You need a psychiatrist"

(The angel who guards heaven
whose face is arrogant and malicious
whose sword burns
points accusingly at me.
I am tired, powerless.
Cannot cry. Cannot speak.
Maria Zaitun is my name.
A hungry and thirsty prostitute.)

Three o'clock in the afternoon.
Sun still burning.
And still no wind.
Maria Zaitun walks on tiptoe
along the burning road.
Suddenly while crossing the street
she slips on dogshit.
She doesn't fall
but the blood flows from an ulcer on her crotch
and trickles to her foot.

Like a cow giving birth
she walks legs wide apart.
Near the market she stops.
Her vision is blurred.
She can scarcely breathe. She is hungry.
People step away from her.
Then she walks behind a restaurant.
Gathers scraps of food from a bin.
Wraps them carefully in a banana leaf
and walks away out of town.

(The angel who guards heaven
whose face is cold and malicious
and whose sword burns
points accusingly at me.
O God, hear me.
Maria Zaitun is my name.
A weak whore, trembling with fear.)

Four o'clock in the afternoon.
She walks like a snail.
The bundle of food-scraps is still in her hand
not yet eaten.
She is covered in sweat.
Her hair is straggly.
Her face is thin and pale
like a dry lemon.

Then it is five o'clock.
She has left the town.
The road is no longer asphalt
just dirt.

She looks at the sun
and slowly says "Stinker!"
After walking another kilometer
she leaves the main road
and turns into the rice-fields
walking on the dividing walls.

(The angel who guards paradise
whose face is superior and malicious
and whose sword burns
drives me away.
Viciously
he thrusts his virile sword
into my crotch.
Hear me, O Lord.
Maria Zaitun my name.
A defeated whore.
A wretched whore.)

Six o'clock in the evening.
Maria Zaitun arrives at the river.
The wind blows.
The sun is setting.
It is twilight.
Wearily she lies down at the edge of the river.
She washes her feet, hands and face.

Then slowly eats.
Stopping after a moment.
Her body is weak
But she has no appetite.
Then she drinks from the river.

(Guarding angel
Can't you feel that twilight has arrived
the wind come down from the mountain
the day lay down its body?
The angel who guards paradise
resolutely drives me away.
He stands like a statue.
And his sword burns.)

Seven o'clock. And night arrives.
Insects buzz.
The river strikes against rocks.
The trees and shrubs on both sides of the river
stand still
and shine in the moonlight.
Maria Zaitun is no longer afraid.
She remembers her childhood and youth.
Bathing in the river with her mother.
Climbing trees.
And fishing with her sweetheart.
She is no longer lonely.
And her fear has gone.
She feels as if she is with an old friend.
But then she wants to tell
the rest of her life's story.
And because she is aware of the failure it has been
She is sad.
And complains to her friend
sobbing all the time.
Which is not good for her heart.

(The angel who guards paradise
whose face is cold and malicious
refuses to hear my reply.
To see my eyes.
It is pointless to speak to him.
Arrogantly he stands.
And his sword burns.)

Time.
Moon.
Trees.
River.
Ulcers
Syphilis
Woman.
Like glass.
River reflecting the bright light.
Long grass shining.

A man comes across the river.
He calls out: "Maria Zaitun, is that you?"
"Yes," Maria Zaitun answers in surprise.
The man crosses the river.
He is strong and handsome.
His hair is curly and his eyes are large.
Maria Zaitun's heart beats faster.
She feels she has known this man.
Though doesn't know where.
Certainly not in bed.
Which is a pity. For she likes men like him.
"So here we meet," the man says.
Maria Zaitun does not know what to say.

For a moment she is surprised.
The man bends and kisses her lips.
He tastes like coconut milk.
She has never known a kiss like that.
Then he opens her brassiere.
She is powerless and indeed pleased.
She surrenders.
With her eyes closed
she feels as if she is sailing
on some sea she has never known.
And when it is finished
she says lovingly:
"I never thought this could happen to me
except in a dream.
I had never dared hope
that a man as handsome as you
might pass through my life."
With great delight he looks at her.
Then smiles, respectfully and patiently.
"What is your name?" Maria Zaitun asks.
"The bride-groom," he replies.
"Show me. You're joking."
And as she says so
Maria Zaitun kisses the man's body all over.
Suddenly she stops.
She has found scars in the body of her hero.
In his left side.
In both hands.
In both feet.
Maria Zaitun slowly says:
"I know who you are."
Then looks directly at the man.
He nods his head. "Indeed. Yes."

(The angel who guards paradise
whose face is wicked and malicious
and whose sword burns
can do nothing.
Clumsily he freezes.
He no longer dares point at me.
I am not afraid now.
My loneliness and misery have been destroyed.
Dancing I enter the gates of paradise
and eat as many apples as I want.
Maria Zaitun is my name.
whore and bride both.)

Sermon

Fantastic.
One hot Sunday
in a church full of people
a young priest stood at the pulpit.
His face was beautiful and holy
his eyes sweet like a rabbit's
and he lifted up both his hands
which were lovely like a lily
and said:
"Now let us disperse.
There is no sermon today."

No one budged.
They sat crowded in their pews.
Many people were standing as well.
They stiffened. Refused to move.
Their eyes filled with questions.
Their mouths hung open
as they stopped praying
but everyone wanted to hear him.
Then all at once they complained
and together with the strange voice from their mouths
came a foul stench
which had to be quickly stifled.

"You can see I am still young.
Allow me to care for my own soul.
Please go away.
Allow me to praise holiness.
I want to go back to the monastery
and meditate on the glory of God."

Again they complained.
No one moved.
Their faces looked sad.
Their eyes were filled with questions.
Their mouths gaped
wanting very much to hear him.

"This people ask for guidance. Lord
God, why have you left me at this moment?
Like a flock of hungry lazy jackals
they open their mouths.
It is hot. I piss in my pants.
Father. Father. Why hast Thou forsaken me?"

Still no one moved.
Their faces were wet.
Their hair was wet.
Their whole bodies were wet.
Sweat poured onto the floor
because it was so hot
and of the misery they bore.
The stench was extraordinarily foul.
And their questions too stank foully.

"My brothers, children of the heavenly father.
This is my sermon.
My very first sermon.
Life is very difficult.
Dark and difficult.
There are many torments.
So in this regard
the wise way to live is ra-ra-ra.
Ra-ra-ra, hum-pa-pa, ra-ra-ra.
Look at the wisdom of the lizard
a creature God loves.
Go close to the ground.
For:
Your souls are squeezed between rocks.
Green.
Mossy.
Like a lizard ra-ra-ra.
Like a centipede hum-pa-pa."

They all spoke together:
Ra-ra-ra. Hum-pa-pa.
Everyone in the church shouted:
Ra-ra-ra. Hum-pa-pa.

"To the men who like guns
who fix the flags of truth to their bayonet-points
I want you to listen carefully
to lu-lu-lu, la-li-lo-lu.
Lift your noses high
so you don't see the people you trample.
For in this way li-li-li, la-li-lo-lu.

"Cleanse the blood from your hands
so as not to frighten me
then we can sit and drink tea
and talk of the sufferings of society
and the nature of life and death.
Life is full of misery and sin.
Life is a big cheat.
La-la-la, li-li-li, la-li-lo-lu.
So let us shoot the sun
Taking aim as carefully as can be."

The people answered him joyfully:
La-la-la, li-li-li, la-li-lo-lu
They stood. They banged their feet against the floor.
Stamping rhythmically and together.
Uniting their voices in:
La-la-la, li-li-li, la-li-lo-lu.
Carried along in the strength of their unity
they shouted together
precisely and rhythmically:
La-la-la, li-li-li, la-li-lo-lu.

"Now we live again.
Feel the force of the blood flowing in you.
In your heads. In your necks. In your breasts.
In your stomachs. Throughout the rest of your bodies.
See my fingers shaking with life.
The blood is bong-bong-bong.
The blood of life is bang-bing-bong.
The blood of the common life is bang-bing-bong-bong.
Life must be lived in a noisy group.
Blood must mix with blood.
Bong-bong-bong. Bang-bing-bong."

The people exploded with the passion of their lives.
They stood on the pews.
Banged with their feet.
They pounded on the bells and the gong
the doors and the windows.
With the one rhythm
In accompaniment to their joyous shouts of:
Bong-bong-bong. Bang-bing-bong.

"We must exalt love.
Love in the long grass.
Love in the shops of Arabs.
Love in the backyard of the church.
Love is unity and tra-la-la.
Tra-la-la. La-la-la. Tra-la-la.
Like the grass
we must flourish
in unity and love.
Let us pulverize ourselves.
Let us shelter beneath the grass.
Taking as our guide:
Tra-la-la. La-la-la. Tra-la-la."

The whole congregation roared.
They began to dance. Following the one rhythm.
They rubbed their bodies against each other.
Men against women. Men against men.
Women with women. Everyone rubbed their bodies.
And some rubbed their bodies against the walls of the church.
And they shouted in a strange mad voice
shrilly and together:
Tra-la-la. La-la-la. Tra-la-la.

"Through the holy prophet Moses
God has said:
Thou must not steal.
Junior civil servants stop stealing carbon paper.
Servant-girls stop stealing fried chicken bones.
Leaders stop stealing petrol.
And girls, stop stealing your own virginity.
Of course, there is stealing and stealing.
The difference is: cha-cha-cha, cha-cha-cha.
All things come from God.
Everything is meant to be shared.
Everything belongs to everyone
Everything is for everyone.
We must be united. Us for us.
Cha-cha-cha, cha-cha-cha.
This is the guiding principle."

They roared like animals:
Grrr-grrr-grrr. Hura.
Cha-cha-cha, cha-cha-cha.
They stole the windowpanes.
They took everything in the church.
The candelabra. The curtains. The carpets.
The silverware. And the statues covered with jewels.
Cha-cha-cha, they sang:
Cha-cha-cha over and over again.
They destroyed the whole church.
Cha-cha-cha.
Like wet panting animals
running to-and-fro.
Cha-cha-cha. Cha-cha-cha.
Then suddenly an old woman screamed:

"I am hungry. Hungrry. Hu-u-unggrryyy."
And suddenly everyone felt hungry.
Their eyes burned.
And they kept shouting cha-cha-cha.

"Because we are hungry
let us disperse.
Go home. Everyone stop."

Cha-cha-cha, they said
and their eyes burned.

"Go home.
The mass and the sermon are over."

Cha-cha-cha, they said.
They didn't stop
They pressed forward.
The church lay in ruins. And their eyes burned.

"Lord. Remember the sufferings of Christ.
We are all his honored sons.
Hunger must be overcome by wisdom."

Cha-cha-cha.
They advanced and beat against the pulpit.
Cha-cha-cha.
They dragged the priest from the pulpit.
Cha-cha-cha.
They tore his robes.
Cha-cha-cha.
A fat woman kissed his fine mouth.

An old woman licked his pure breast.
And girls pulled at both his legs.
Cha-cha-cha.
And thus they raped him in a noisy throng.

Cha-cha-cha.
Then they chopped his body to bits.
Everyone ate his flesh. Cha-cha-cha.
They feasted in the strength of their unity.
They drank his blood.
They sucked the marrow from his bones.
Until they had eaten everything
and there was nothing left.
Fantastic

Suto's Song for Fatima

Twenty-three suns
rise from your shoulders.
Your body smells of the earth
and my soul bursts into flames.
The sky is like a blue tetron cloth
stretched out
shining and sparkling
refusing to accept the sad window of my mind.
My spirit and yours
are like proton and electron
seething
seething
beneath twenty-three suns.
Twenty-three suns
burning away my sadness.

Fatima's Song for Suto

The net on my bed is back
my fate rests on the pillow.
When you speak
my heart enters yours.

Sadness knocks at my window
from the earth beneath the roses.
When you were born you were naked and unknowing
yet life is more than a marketplace.

A Poem About Condors

The mountain wind moves softly through the forest,
sweeps across the wide river,
and finally comes to rest among the tobacco leaves.
Sadly it watches
the weary pace of the farm laborers
as they march across the rich earth,
which offers them only poverty.

The farm laborers work hard,
they live in dark shacks,
planting seed in the fertile ground,
bringing in the abundant harvest,
leading lives of misery.

They harvest for landlords
who live in huge palaces.
Their sweat falls like gold
for the carpetbaggers who run cigar factories in Europe.
When they demand their share of the profits,
the economists straighten their ties,
and send them condoms.

My people's faces are lined with pain.
They move like ghosts,
from morning to night,
reaching out,
turning this way and that,
finding nothing.
By sunset, their bodies are pulp.

At night they lie on the floor, exhausted,
and their souls turn into condors.

Hundreds of condors,
millions of condors,
moving to the high mountains,
where they can rest in silence.
Only in silence
can they fully savor their pain and bitterness.

The condors scream.
They scream with rage
as they escape to the lonely mountains.

The condors scream,
and their screams echo among the rocks
and the silent mountains.

Millions of condors clawing at rocks,
pecking at rocks, pecking at the air.
In town, men prepare to shoot them.

I Hear the Sound

I hear the sound
of wounded, screaming animals.

There are men shooting at the moon.
There are birds falling from their nests.

It is time to rise.
To bear witness.
To protect life.

A Pile of Corn

A pile of corn in a room
and a young man
of limited schooling.

Staring at the corn,
the young man sees a field;
he sees farmers,
he sees harvest time
and on the dawn of a particular day,
women with bundles in slings
heading toward market...
And he also sees
on a particular morning
young women laughing
near the well
as they pound the kernels of corn
to flour.
While in the kitchen
hearths flame.
In the pure air
he catches the scent of corn cakes.

A pile of corn in the room
and a young man.
He is ready to work on the corn.
He sees the possibility
brain and hand
are ready to work.

Or this:

A pile of corn in a room
and a young graduate from senior high.
Without the money, college is out of reach
All he has is a pile of corn in his room.

He stares at the corn
and he sees himself suffering.
He sees himself thrown out of the discotheque.
He sees a sharp pair of shoes in the store window.
He sees his rival on a motorcycle.
He sees lottery numbers.
He sees himself poor, a failure.
A pile of corn in the room
has no bearing on reason
will not provide him help.

A pile of corn in the room
will not help a young man
whose view of life comes from books
and not from life.
One not trained to analyze,
and able only to memorize conclusions.
One who's only been trained to be a user
but with little training in self-reliance.
Education has separated him from life.

I ask you:
What is the use of education
if it only makes a person feel foreign
amid the facts of life?
What is the use of education
if it only pushes a person
to become a kite in the capital city
and awkward in one's home village?
What is the use of a person studying
philosophy, literature, technology, medicine
or whatever,
if in the end,
when he goes home to the village, he can only say:
"I feel foreign and lonely here!"

A Poem About a Girl and Her Employer

Don't put your arms around me like that.
I know what comes next.
I'm no fortune-teller
but I know
what you're after...

I wasted my time at school.
They taught me maths, typing, languages,
hygiene and civics.
But not what to do
when the boss sneaks up behind me
and puts his arms around me.

Please don't put your arms around me.
Even my boyfriend doesn't do that.
I know what you want.
I know what it means
when your arms brush against my breasts...

They taught me to hate sin
but forgot to teach me
how to find a job.
They taught me to live
in a world of unnatural machinery.
They taught me to need things
the bosses make
and control.
Hair-driers, air conditioners,
synthetic vitamins, tonics,
soft drinks and high school diplomas.

Education bound me
to their markets, to their money.
And now that I have grown up
where can I run–
except to the world of the bosses?

Don't put your arms around me.
I'm no intellectual
but I know
that all the work I do at my desk
only leads to one thing.
Don't! Please don't, sir!
Please don't put your arms around me!
Ah. Hm.
The money you put in my bra
is my school certificate.
Oh. Yes.
I see.
You're hurting me.
Your fat belly
is pushing against mine.
Your stinking mouth
is kissing mine.
It all seems quite normal
to you.
Society helps you.
They hold my legs.
Force my thighs apart
As you climb on top of me.

A Poem About a Family Photograph

On the fifteenth day of the year of the moon.
A saffron-powdered face shines in the sky.
A cold dry winter walks down a dusty road.
A small snake is eaten by a dragon.
A dove is lost from its nest.

The father tells his friends:

Things will be fine. Sure they will.
There's no point in grumbling.
Life isn't meant to be easy;
not that it ever was.
We're not too badly off.
The family has all it needs,
a house, and a car,
they can't complain.
The kids are doing well at school;
the girl's in high school, the boy's at university.
We've got a color TV, orchids
and air-conditioning. Religion.
Yes, you could say we've made it.
No use making a fuss,
could get you into trouble.
Only fools protest, it doesn't do any good.
A man could even lose his job.

*

On the fifteenth day of the year of the moon,
The dry wind hangs in the branches of the bitter-mango tree.
Night is welcomed by soft voices in the grass,
Dogs peer into rubbish bins.
Cats walk on rooftops.
And scorpions wait under rocks.

His wife sits at her dressing table and says:

The days flow like wine.
The air is full of opium.
Nothing's very clear any more.
The days fly past like shadows.
You can't believe in anything at all.
My husband is always out in his car.
He's always spending money.
The more we have, the more we owe.
The children's school fees are always late.
Good Lord, what will happen to them?
Will they turn out to be just like him?
That man!
He used to live simply when he was young,
he used to think for himself too.
But now everything seems wrong.
Everything annoys him.
Everything is so expensive
and he's never satisfied.
He's always fiddling with the TV,
even when there's nothing wrong,
then he just sits there and goes to sleep.
The noise doesn't seem to bother him.
I wish he'd smile sometimes.

He gets mad at the car
and mad at the television
He gets high blood pressure, I'll tell you that.
Food doesn't interest him,
he's diabetic, you know...
I'm always doing the wrong thing.
He gets mad at me because he can't get mad at anyone else.
He's a failure and won't admit it.
A drifter and a coward.
A man who won't stand up and fight.

*

On the fifteenth day of the year of the moon.
Seven birds sleep in a jackfruit tree.
While a snake searches beneath them for food.
The river whispers in the distance.
Crocodiles sleep on its broken banks.
Two crabs make love among the rocks.

The daughter says:

Marry me. Make me pregnant.
Take me away. I want to be your slave.
I hate it here.
I'm always wrong, Everyone gets mad at me,
Father gets mad because of his car and the TV
Mother gets mad because she's mad at Father.
The house is always tidy
but I feel so uncomfortable.
Of course they love me.
But what's it all for?

What are they living for?
Is Father only living for his car and television?
Is Mother only living because she doesn't know
what else she can do?
And what about me? What am I going to be?
I've been in school for thirteen years
and I still can't stand on my own two feet.
What do we want out of life?
To eat? Read comics?
What?
I guess it's not worth bothering about.
We are all too busy.
Darling, help me rob a bank.
Shoot some morphine into my breast, honey.

*

On the fifteenth day of the year of the moon.
The rooftops shine brightly
in the moonlight.
A well stands black under a tree.
Bamboo roots shine brightly.
Bats sweep back and forth.
A skink attacks a grasshopper.

The son sits at his desk writing a letter:

Dear Mom and Dad,
I'm going, Leaving home.
You've been good to me.
But I don't want to live the way you do.
I won't worship wealth.

I won't spend my life
pursuing useless luxuries.
You're rich,
but not secure.
Dad tells me to play it cool;
he just drifts with the tide,
this way and that.
You have social status,
but no one respects you.
What right do you have to the things you own?
Did you work for them? Doing what?
What work does a corrupt bureaucrat do?
A peasant is more productive.
A laborer serves society better.
You make rules.
You serve your superiors.
You keep the rulers and the people apart.
You're destructive, not productive.
You don't deserve the large salary they pay you!
Have you ever protested at injustice?
Have you? Never!
It's too risky, isn't it!
Do you want me to be like you?
I'm disgusted by the example you've set me.
Mom and Dad, goodbye.
I'm too strong not to want to be free.

A Poem for a Student Meeting

For the students of the University of Indonesia

The sun rose this morning,
smelt baby piss on the horizon,
saw brown rivers crawling to the sea,
and heard bees buzzing in the forest.

Now the sun stands at an angle of sixty degrees.
It is a witness to our gathering
and our discussions.

We ask:
Why do good intentions so often go astray?
Why are good intentions so often in conflict?
They say: "We want the best."
And we ask: "The best for whom?"

Some are winners and some are losers,
some have guns and some have bruises,
some sit up and some sit down,
some are rich and some go begging round the town.
We want to know:
"Best for whom?
Whose side are you on?"

Why is it that the better the intentions,
the more peasants lose their land
and the more city-folk own country estates?
Large plantations

benefit small groups of people.
Imported modern machinery
cannot farm tiny plots of land.

So naturally we ask them
whose interests you have at heart.

The sun is higher now.
Soon it will rule above our heads.
It is hot. We want to know
whom we're being taught to support.
Is our learning
a means of freedom
or oppression?

Before long the sun will start to set.
Night will return.
The lizards will call out from the walls.
The moon will sail across the sky.
But our questions will not disappear.
They will live in your dreams.
And grow in your back gardens.

Tomorrow
the sun will rise again.
One new day after another.
Our questions will become a forest.
They will enter the rivers
be waves on the ocean.

Under today's sun we ask:
Some are sleeping and some are weeping,
some are cruel and some are fools.
We want the best.
Whose side are we on?

A Poem About a Bottle of Beer

Draining a bottle of beer,
looking at the world,
and seeing lots of hungry people.
Burning incense,
smelling the damp earth,
and listening to the riots.

The money spent in town on a single night
could develop ten villages.
What sort of civilization are we supposed to be defending?

Why do we build cities
and forget about our villages?
Why does development mean accumulation
and not distribution?

Our cities are not based on industry,
but on the needs of foreign industrial nations for markets
and raw materials.
Our cities
provide the infrastructure for Europe, Japan, China, America,
    Australia and other industrial nations to accumulate
    wealth.

Where are the old roads
which used to link one village to another?
They have been neglected.

Turned into sewers and rubbish dumps.
Today's highways
follow blueprints of former colonial carriageways.
They allow goods to flow from the docks to the provinces,
    and raw materials to flow from the provinces
    back to the docks.
The highways have been specially built,
not for the farmers,
but for middlemen and carpetbaggers.

We are carried along by a civilization we do not control,
in which our only function is to eat and shit,
we are powerless to create anything.
Is this as far as we go?

Do countries progress only through industrialization?
Must we dream of owning factories
which endlessly produce goods–
compulsively produce–
then force still other countries
to become our markets?

*

Is tourism the only alternative to industry?
Can our economic planners see only capitalism and communism?
Why does no one care about our own environment?
Must we be carried along by the forces of accumulation,
    as they spread greed and pollution,
    around us and within?

*

We are dominated by the dream
of becoming other people.
We are strangers
in the land of our ancestors.
Dazed, the villagers chase dreams
and sell themselves to Jakarta.
Dazed, people in Jakarta chase dreams
and sell themselves to Japan,
Europe, and America.

A Poem About Bali

Because we believe in industry,
and are convinced we can make money
from our art and scenery,
we have decided to turn Bali into a tourist resort.

Well then,
let's not kid ourselves about what we're doing
when we open Bali to tourists.
After all, jets exist,
companies buy planes,
airlines need passengers,
and passengers need places to go.
The airlines can compete
to process leisure
and family holidays.

We will shrink Bali,
its art, culture and beauty,
and sell it to the tourists,
wrapped in tinsel.

Jets fly over the forests of Brazil,
past Badui mountain settlements,
appearing in the most unlikely places,
swifter than dreams,
bringing culture shock.

This is a different sort of oppression.
It came so quickly we were taken by surprise.
It came so cunningly we were powerless.

And while we were still dazed,
jet-planes came out of our dreams,
with new forms of financial domination:
hotels serving steak and Coca-Cola;
airports; highways; and sightseers.

"Oh honey, look!
Look at the natives!
He's climbing that palm tree like a monkey!
Isn't he fantastic! Take his photograph!"

*

"Watch out! Don't touch his hand!
Just smile and say hello.
See–his hand is filthy.
He might have lice."

*

"My God, they're so innocent.
The women don't even cover their breasts.
Look, John, what magnificent breasts.
And look at this pair. Wonderful!
The people are so free and spontaneous.
I wish I could be like that...
OK! OK!... I was only joking.
I know you hate it when I don't wear my bra.
All right John, stop complaining!
Stand next to her, dear,
and I'll take your picture.
Ah! Fabulous!"

The World Bank
helps backward nations
with huge projects,
in which ninety per cent of the goods are imported.

We progress like slaves
or middlemen and consumers.

In Bali,
Indonesian-owned hotels fail,
smashed by packaged-tours.
Our folk-culture is destroyed
by the standards of international trade.

Our dances are no longer ceremonies,
they are simply entertainment.
Our carvings do not express our emotions,
they are mere handicrafts.

We live dominated by whim,
forgetful of nature.
We are subject to harsh,
strongly institutionalized rules,
which ignore our hearts,
our livers and kidneys,
the rivers and forests.
In Bali, they spit on us,
our beds, mountains and temples.

A Poem for Joki Tobing From Widuri

Clouds of dust transform the faces of parking attendants.
Anger slackens in the ancient mind.
The poor defy their misery.
Oh, Joki Tobing, I cry out for you,
because your face appears in my dreams.
Oh, Joki Tobing, I cry out for you,
because I am caught in your breathing.
From one city bus to another
you hunt for me.
Seated side by side we witness
the dinginess of life.
Our blood begins to beat more quickly,
when we see a cluster of flowers in bloom,
on top of the rubble of a hopeless age.

A Poem for Widuri From Joki Tobing

Against a backdrop of cardboard huts,
I recall your face.
I stand in front of you
wearing the dust of my poverty.
Wipe my face, Widuri.
My adolescent dreams have fallen
on the field of unemployment.
The Ciliwung River is clouded,
the faces of the fishermen are clouded,
then your loosened hair appears.
Poverty and hunger
give rise to my determination.
Your beautiful face and hair
become the rainbow on my horizon.

A Poem About Old Friends

We look at each other, friend.
Wondering whether
we have ever met.
Standing near the train door,
squeezed among the passengers,
traveling from Yogya to Jakarta,
I watch you, asleep in the aisle
on a pile of newspapers,
holding a child,
with your wife beside you,
suckling a baby.
We once rode the same truck,
on top of a heap of stinking cabbage-heads
fondling the vendors' breasts
and were amazed to see the police stop us
and demand their unofficial toll.
We know each other, friend,
we've traveled the same roads.

*

What sort of a life is this?
People moved from here to there:
not from one set of opportunities to another,
but from one situation
to another, exactly the same.

*

We're side by side now, friend.
You can recognize the smell of my clothes.
Don't worry,
we've met.
It was raining,
I was pulling a sheet of plastic out of a rubbish bin
and so were you.
We looked at each other.
You were carrying a small child on your back.
I opened my mouth
to say something...
and couldn't!
You punched me in the jaw...
Dazed,
I watched you take the piece of plastic
to a cardboard shanty
and fold it over the roof.
You crawled inside with your child
and a bundle of rice you had stolen.
We fought
near a row of stalls
in a bus station.
Yes, friends, we know each other,
we're bastards of the same glorious race.

*

What sort of a life is this?
People selling their bodies in dark parks
so they can have enough to eat.
Teachers' wives selling their bodies in big hotels
so they can park their asses in big cars.

*

Twelve pairs of shining breasts,
with diamonds round their nipples.
And red silk panties
under their skirts.
We can laugh at the memory,
can't we, friend.
Don't worry, we've met.
We were there together.
Watching the elite
licking the women's crotches
and pouring wine over themselves.
We were pimps,
buying our suits in Singapore,
burying our heads in film stars' laps,
playing golf and mahjong,
and dining on crabs and oysters in the best restaurants.

*

Fantasy
and reality
are both the same.
Fantasies come true
and reality is fantasy
in a civilization based on illusion.

*

Come on, admit it,
you recognize my cough.
You've seen me spitting in the gutter.
That's right. Your old friend.

We used to steal your father's car
and take turns in sleeping with his girls.
We used to watch your mother misbehaving
with your father's adjutant.
We used to buy morphine from our teacher.
We used to steal the valium the doctor gave your mother.
Do you remember how we used to collapse
in the main street, Malioboro,
beside the beggars?
We did all that,
the sons of the rich were gods.

*

We used to get
as high as the sky.
Really high.
The state was like ganja…
it kept us high… as the clouds…
We owned the law.
We wrote it with the sweat of our armpits
on the soles of our shoes.
We were rich tramps.
We killed people
to reassure ourselves.

*

It's good to shake hands like old friends.
Good to meet again.
There's no doubt about it,
we've met before.
Couldn't you recognize me
by the way I walk?

We stopped the traffic together,
burnt cars,
waved placards,
and charged forward, demonstrating.
We planned our strategies
in steam baths and restaurants.
We synchronized our gold watches.
We stayed up late, plotting,
in night clubs,
with our arms around the hostesses.
We were young men,
the hope of the nation.

Politics helped us take the world by storm.
Politics helped us get rid of the old, decadent forces.
so we could rule instead.
Politics has helped us get ahead:
to go from trishaws to taxis, our own cars,
then sports cars and helicopters!
Politics means festivals and football.
Politics means lots of art shows.
If anyone bitches too much,
we'll say they were never really heroes.

    *

Where have the fireflies gone?
Why aren't my wooden sandals outside the door?
The times are hard.
I look for my glasses
and can't find them.

    *

Yes, it's me!
No doubt about it.
You've smelt my sweat.
And heard me cough.
We've shaken hands.
It's me all right,

We've stood together
and watched the rainbow turn to tongues of fire,
and the dark mountains glow red-hot,
while private planes flew among the clouds dropping sperm
as those inside watched blue movies.

*

Endless wealth
Endless poverty.
Endless pain.
Endless ridiculous nonsense.
Endless conflicting possibilities.
The flood of voices is slowly rising.
Voices under the desks.
Voices out of drawers.
Voices through the mosque doors.
Eventually
the world will explode in technicolor flames,
flames the color of nylon and plastic,
flames of a thousand different hues.
We are all witnesses
to the same event
and the same set of circumstances.
We do not know what is happening
but it is our common creation.

A Poem About a Guerrilla

for my son, Isaias Sadewa

You are so far away, my darling,
you are bathed in sunlight,
I can see you, high in the sky,
as I bear my rifle and banner.

With your cotton shawl over your head,
among the banana trees in our dusty village.
You are beautiful.
A regiment of the oppressor's tanks
rumble in the distance.

The night is bathed with sunlight.
The burning battleground is a field of green.
As the mortars rain down, my darling,
you are a great and sacred rainbow.

My bullets are spent.
Blood spurts from my chest.
I can hear you,
and my ancestors who have died,
fighting, on behalf of the people,
singing hymns of war.

A Poem by an Old Man Under a Tree

This is my poem,
the poem of an old man standing under a withered tree
with my hands behind my back
and a clove cigarette in my mouth

I'm thinking about the world.
I can see the economy reflected
in the foreign goods carried by the shops,
and the pockmarked roads between villages,
which keep people apart.
I can see greed and corruption.
I spit in disgust.

I'm standing outside the police station.
I see the bleeding face of a demonstrator.
I see force used illegally.
And a long, dusty road,
full of skinny cats,
full of scabby children,
full of ugly, threatening soldiers.

I'm walking in the hot sun,
along a road of stinking, dishonest
development projects.
I hear people saying:
"Human rights are relative.
Political stability is essential
for economic growth.

Some loss of personal freedom
is, of course, inevitable,
if we are to eradicate poverty."
What a lot of water-buffalo shit!
Has farting replaced justice?

We have done away with basic rights;
strengthened the rich and powerful,
destroyed the peasants, laborers,
fishermen, students and journalists.

We legalize lies
and ignore the truth around us.

I hear fast cars.
I hear false accusations.
I hear news of urban guerrillas
running wild in Europe.
A man who worked for the fascists,
who hated the unions,
has been kidnapped
and killed
by a group of angry men.

I watch the sun setting over the harbor.
My feet are sore,
my cigarette's gone out again.
I can see blood in the sky.
Violence is becoming more attractive.
Society is increasingly oppressed.

Angry men are starting to take out their weapons.
It takes a hoodlum to stop a hoodlum.
The temptation is growing.
If the courts will not act against government hoodlums,
common hoodlums will.
What will conscience say then?
Who created this state of emergency?
Must the people imitate these official hoodlums?
If not, why isn't something done about them?
What does conscience say?

What a vivid sunset!
So brief and yet so lovely.
Soon we will start looking for the moon and stars.

How transitory it all is.
The sky within us is dead,
the sky beyond us is blurred by the sunset,
our consciences are blurred by lies.

Yes, I'm an old man.
I'm tired, but I'm not ready to die.
I'm standing at the crossroads.
I can feel myself turning into a dog.
But something in me still wants to write poetry,
like a human being

A Poem About Eyes

There are whisperings underground.
There is conflict on the surface.
There is confusion between the houses.
There is uncertain weeping in the rice fields.
And, heh! Right behind me!
There are angry soldiers too.

What is happening? I don't know.

I see sudden bursts of flame.
I see signs.
None of it makes any sense.
I see anguished faces,
unable to speak
and I am worried.

What is happening? I don't know.

Sights and sounds
weigh in upon us,
oppressing us.
This is happening because what happened, happened,
and I didn't know it had happened.
I didn't know. You didn't know.
Nobody knew.

There was no way we could know.
The newspapers are censored,
free speech is strictly regulated.

The newspapers used to be our eyes.
Now we have official eyes.
We no longer see complex truths,
but colored slides of economic miracles,
stitched together by the emperor's tailors.

The people's eyes have been ripped out.
They grope among rumors.
The government's eyes are also threatened.
Protected by dark glasses,
the government sits isolated behind its big desk.
The government's eyes have been replaced
by spies.

Spies are expensive.
They eat a lot.
They are hard to control.
They speak like carthorses
wearing blinkers.

In the half-light,
everyone looks angry.
The people are angry. The government is angry.
They are all angry because they have no eyes.
Their eyes have been sabotaged.
The only eyes still in circulation
belong to spies.

Poor People

Poor people in the roads,
living in the gutters.
They have lost their battles.
They are tantalized by their dreams.
You must not forget them.

The wind carries the smell of their clothing.
Their damp hair clings to the full moon.
Legions of pregnant women in the sky
bear fruit conceived by the roadside.

Poor people. Sinful people.
Carrying dark babies. Grass and moss beside the highway.
You must not neglect them.

If you push them away,
your roads will be haunted by shadows.
Your sleep will be broken by nightmares.
Your children will use words you do not understand.

Do not say we are a rich country
there are too many poor people in the cities and towns.
Do not say you are rich,
if your neighbors eat cats.
Our national symbols should be wooden clogs and calico.
No one should have to dress like a Dutchman,
wear a tie, to meet the President.
The army should not be allowed to beat up students.

Poor people in the roads
will enter your sleep.
Women of the streets
will feed your sons.
Dirty hands
will grope at your windows.
You will not be able to stop them.

Make no mistake: they do exist.
They will be the perpetual challenge
to your ideology.
Their yellow teeth
will laugh at your religion.
TB and syphilis from the squalid lanes
will hang on the curtains of the President's palace
and the catalogues of the art galleries.

The poor stretch endlessly back into history;
always present, like the heat
and the threat of rain.
The poor take up their knives
and point them at us,
or themselves.
Remember this:
the poor
are Abraham's children too.

An Angry Poem

Because we eat roots
and you have lots of wheat in your barns...
Because we live crowded together
and you have more room than you need...
we cannot be friends.

Because we live in the dark
and you live in the light...
Because we live in poverty
and you have locks on your doors...
we do not trust you.

Because we wander the streets
and you live in comfort...
Because our shacks are flooded
and you have parties on leisure yachts...
we do not like you.

Because we are silenced
and you can say whatever you like...
Because we are threatened
and you have the power...
we say NO to you.

Because we have no choices
and you draw up development plans...
Because we wear sandals
and you wear guns...

Because we must be respectful
and you control the prisons...
we say NO! and NO! to you.

Because we are flowing rivers
and you are unfeeling rocks,
water shall wear away the rocks.

A Bat

Dazed by the traffic lights
I bend to look at my shoes.
I am swaying like a bat.
Neither happy nor sad.
Drifting in time.
Ma, I see you at every junction.
I never knew that you could fill
the pages of my address book so completely.

I am walking again.

Should I telephone a friend?
Should I eat prawns at a restaurant?
I am angry with intellectuals who refuse to bear witness.
They disguise serious social problems as metaphysics.
A strong soul becomes a myth faced with an armored vehicle.
You are the only one I can talk with.

I drag my feet through rubbish.

I want to write more poems.
My determination cannot be killed so easily.
Come here, Ma, here into my coat pocket.
You are my will to live, all I hope for.

New Year's Poem, 1990

After the financiers conspire with the tyrants,
after human rights in poor countries have been oppressed
for the greatness of developed nations,
what is the face of humanity?

On the street people are drugged by the miracle of advertisements
at home they are tense, angry and deceitful.
Dreams replace plans.
Upgrading replaces awareness.

Metropolitan cities of the third world
are arteries
from the heart of the developed word.
Arteries that will become cancerous
that will kill the life force of villages
and finally, with no chance of self-determination,
become evil, contemptible and dangerous.
That is accumulation without distribution.

Without human rights there is no certainty of life.
People can only be moved by outside forces
for they have lost the power to move themselves.
They are pigs in a pen
alienated from their own lives.
The people have become dunces
with no opinions of their own.
In school students are taught to memorize
humming like bees in a hive
and finally become unemployed scholars.

In places of prayer people flap their lips in endless repetition
and in villages they are filled with hate
become skilled in killing and burning.
The bureaucrats are sick from high blood pressure
they repeat what they have been told, like radios.
Why does development not mean progress?
Why does the wealth of one country
yield poverty for its neighbor?

The culture of accumulation cannot be defended.
Look at the traffic jams, pollution and erosion!
What does the accumulation of power mean
if your life is filled with distrust
and you live in fear of vengeance?
What does the accumulation of wealth mean
if the rotten smell of poverty
seeps in through your bedroom window?
Isolation breeds only loneliness
without calm.
Another person's wounds are your wounds too.

The culture of distribution cannot be developed
in the absence of human rights.
What is the meaning of nature's wealth
without the application of human effort?
How can human effort be encouraged
without developing an awareness
of personal responsibility
towards nature
and one's fellow beings?

Weary faces
are reflected in the gutter water
and in the coffee cups of financiers.
The musty smell of sodden dreams
spreads through the red light districts
and the stock market.

Seriously.
What use is it for you to be great in this life
if in the end you are afraid to die
because you have betrayed your soul for so long?

An Old Man's Poem About Bandung, "A Sea of Fire"

How could we have had a state
if we couldn't defend our own territory?
How could we be a people
if we couldn't defend our life together?

That was why
cunningly
we surrendered Bandung to the British
and then burned it to the ground
turning our beloved city into a sea of fire.
Now my soul remembers
the quivering waves of heat,
the smell of smoke, of sweat,
the explosions bouncing against the orange clouds
and the dark red horizon.

We fought
for the right to live with dignity.
Our sovereignty was the basis for equal justice.
How could we experience that
under colonial oppression?
What people
would allow their descendents to live
without these guarantees?

---

*) On March 23, 1946, residents of the city of Bandung and the retreating Indonesian
Republican forces set fire to the city rather than surrender it in response to a British
ultimatum. The event is known by the words "*Bandung Lautan Api*" or "Bandung, A
Sea of Fire."

True life must be ours to control
to shape and develop
to defend.
That was why we fought oppression.
Bandung was in flames
But our sovereignty was secure.

I am old now.
I lie awake at midnight
in the mountains.
What is that smell?
Smoke from old battlefields
carried by my dreams?
Or the stench of a modern industrial cesspit?
What is the sound I hear?
The din of old battles in Priangan?
Or the noisy chaos of modern life
betrayed by unjust gods?

I am startled. Confused. Have I been woken
by my dreams?
Have I been startled
by signs of life?
In the stillness of the night,
I call out to you, my sons and daughters!
What is happening?

The blood of my friends
was shed in Sukakarsa,
Dayeuh Kolot,
Kiara Condong,
across every battlefield.

Now
we are all startled, unable to sleep.
My sons and daughters, what is happening?
Can you answer our common question?

Oh, my old warrior friends,
are we still prepared to fight
for mutual justice?

People of every historical generation
will experience sudden periods of wakefulness
in the lonely silence of the night
when they face these same questions:
What is happening?
What has happened?
What are you doing now?
The meaning of our brief existence
will be determined by the answers
we give to these questions.

For the People of Rangkasbitung ^{*)}

Ladies and gentlemen,
good evening.
My name is Multatuli.
I come from the past.
I was a Dutch civil servant,
appointed to administer Rangkasbitung,
the capital of Lebak at that time.
It was a difficult experience.
The people were oppressed by their own Regent.
They could sweat
but dare not laugh.
Their personal rights had been violated.
For the sake of the colonizers.
The Netherlands colluded with this evil.
I tried to stop it and could not.
I was defeated and powerless.

I witnessed
justice conquered
by the powerful
in sophisticated and audacious ways.
Without showing the slightest malice.

---

*) "Multatuli" was the pen name of Eduard Douwes Dekker, author of the 19th century novel, *Max Havelaar or The Coffee Auctions of the Dutch Trading Company*. The novel was deeply critical of the Dutch colonial system and of the corrupt Javanese nobles who took extensive advantage of the system for their own benefit. Saijah and Adinda, the subjects of the following two poems, are characters in the seventeenth chapter of the novel, although their stories are rather different from those presented here.

They proclaimed their unjust decrees
in the most precise language,
and politely divided their profits,
extracted from the masses,
who had lost their land and livestock.
All this was done
as if it were completely natural.

On Sundays, our people in Holland
dressed in their best clothes
and diligently prayed.
Then they had lunch.
We Dutch were a polite race.
our families never swore,
our grammar was always correct,
we were proud of the huge profits
drawn from the coffee trade,
efficiently produced through forced labor
in our colony.
Feeling dignified and proud,
we spoke about the success
of our rule and our colonies.
Yes, we always washed our hands before meals
And balanced our sherbet on our laps.
With the same dignity
we sent our marines
to slaughter the islanders of Maluku
and the peasants of Java
who tried to defend
their own sovereignty.
Yes, we are a people
who never forgot to wash our hands.

We are weary when we contemplate
the state of humanity
today.
Once the Dutch uttered the same complaints
when they spoke of their subjection
to the Spanish.
They cursed the oppressive Prince Alba.
Were they any better
than that evil ruler?

I am sure that I was not the only one
who regretted the black marks
that stained our faith.
Honest thought failed
because it could not be fulfilled
in honest dealings.
Time continued to pass
and showed the increasing extent of the problem.
We could not be fair
and create the opportunities
we proclaimed.
Our thoughts were complex and subtle
but we were not yet free,
there were too many obstacles
and too little time.
How could we administer justice
when our minds were always confused?
I think we were tired.
But we should not stop at this point.

Isn't justice here, today,
as bad as it was under colonialism?
In those days, the people of Rangkasbitung
had no legal rights
in the presence of the Adipati of Lebak.
Do they have any more rights
in the presence of our modern day lords?
Once the Adipati of Lebak
could escape the law.
Can we bring today's greedy and cruel lords
before the courts?
Perfect freedom
belongs to the nation and its citizens.
Your nation is independent
but are its citizens free?
Can a people with no legal rights
ever be free?

The leaders of advanced nations weep
when they speak to their sons
about "democracy".
Then they casually lift the phone,
as they sit beside their swimming pools
and give their support to overseas tyrants
in order to create huge profits
for their own people.

Oh, Lord God!
My whole body feels weak
as I say this.

I am trying to stand up,
but my bones will not support my body.
I am fighting my sense of futility.
I see advanced nations
offering economic aid
to the poor.
As a result,
citizens in developing nations
lose their land
so that rich men can play golf,
so that dams can be built
to generate electricity
for foreign-owned factories.
And for each meter of land
the wretched subjects
receive sufficient compensation
to buy a packet of American cigarettes.

Perhaps my presence here
is beginning to make you feel uncomfortable?
It was like that in the past.
Are people like myself
too aware of history?
But remember:
although history always gives birth
to injustices,
it also gives birth
to people like me.
When I realize that
I no longer feel useless.

Gentlemen, rulers of the world,
we both understand history.
For better or worse,
you cannot deny
I exist.
My name is Multatuli.
I am not a book
to be banned or burned.
I am not a wall
to be knocked down.
I am Multatuli.
part of your conscience.
I cannot be flattened
like a field.

Gentlemen, rulers of the world,
if the situation is already wretched,
do you have the right to make it worse?
Basically this is the question history asks
all of you.
Ladies and gentlemen present here today,
now that I understand history,
I do not feel so lonely.
My feelings of futility are irrelevant,
because now I know my duty.
Which is: to be and continue to grow.
Ladies and gentlemen,
I thank you.

Saijah's Song for Adinda

Adinda! Adinda!
I was robbed on the way.
They stabbed me in the belly, back and neck.
They stole all my savings.

Oh God!
I was only a few kilometers from the village,
Bearing ten years of longing.
My dreams have faded.
My hopes have slipped from my hands.

Adinda! Adinda!
Poverty separated us.
For ten years I restrained my desire.
Love is difficult in a time gone mad,
a life full of threat.
Rights are always wrong.
I had nothing, I was trash.
The conquered are wretched.
Although I was poor and powerless
I did the best I could,
I was afraid I might go mad,
afraid of sin.

But now,
after earning what we needed,
I was thrown into a swamp.
My longing and hopes have been crushed.
My body cannot hold my soul.
The poor are betrayed by the poor.

Adinda! Adinda!
Is that you I see, coming through the mist?
Is it you, is it death?
I want to make love to you!
My body reaches out
I remember your face.
My mouth is dry with passion.
I see your naked body in the sky.
Butterflies caress my crotch.
My hands reach out to touch your breasts.
Adinda!
A thousand fireflies
adorn your long loose hair
and touch my face,
as your body comes down from the sky
and presses against me.
Then I feel your tongue
enter my mouth.
And as a truck loaded with wheat
roars past,
my seed flows.
Then, slowly,
very slowly,
my soul vanishes,
together with your image.

Adinda's Song for Saijah

I sing to myself in Kalijodo.
A love song like a tree without leaves.
Carrying my grief like a tree without roots.
Night waiting for dawn.

Saijah, darling!
Without your clear guidance
my shabby love song beats out
searching for you.

Ten years ago
my song was strong and firm.
But now it is embarrassed
and filled with shame.

Darling, I have sinned.
Powerless to resist, I stained our love.

Soon after you went to Sumatra
I was restless, trapped by my longing.
Each month the full moon shone,
I saw your face.
I felt I was going mad.

Each month my longing intensified.
My nipples itched.
The skin on my belly tickled.
Rivers of blood pounded through my body.
I sighed and panted loudly.
It was hard for my heart to beat
so far from you.

One day,
overwhelmed by my longing for you,
I met a man in the village square.
He was like a father to me.
He was a roadworks supervisor.
An important man in our poor village.
He liked to share his cigarettes.
And had work to offer.
He was a friendly man
his words were easy.
At that time I was selling sticky rice cakes,
fried bananas, rice and vegetables.
He always bought my left over stock.
And shared it with his workers.
I was attracted by his money
and his fatherly ways.
He often encouraged me
to follow you to Sumatra.
When he embraced me
behind the banana trees
his hands were warm and pleasant
and he made me feel better.

Then your letter arrived from Menggala.
You said that you wanted to open land in Karta.
I was confused, crazy.
My chest was a furnace, my desire burned like coals.
I told the Supervisor everything.
He put his arms around me again.
I felt better when he said:
"Get ready,

I'll take you to Saijah
In a week's time."

My God, I'd never left the village.
The door to my prison swung open.
The vast world outside tempted me.

The whole village gave me their blessing
when we left to go to Sumatra.
He held my hand in the bus.
I forgot about my poverty and misery.
We sped towards the sun.

What did I know about Sumatra?
But I had a guide, I had a father.
He invited me to stop over in Karawaci.

That night he knocked on my door.
He gave me a skirt, a shawl and blouse.
As I was overwhelmed with delight,
he embraced me, pressing his body against me,
my firm breasts against his chest,
making my blood pound.
I couldn't say "no".
I was drunk with passion
when he kissed my face and neck.

That night he took my maidenhood.
His strength crushed my awareness.

My darling, since that night in Karawaci,
I have stained our love many times.
I have touched sin
and held it against my breast.
I have enjoyed the intoxication of the world.

That night
as I lay confused,
listening to him snoring beside me,
I resolved to give myself,
body and soul, to this man.

I thought I could be his wife.
He only wanted to be my boss.
He enjoyed me for a month.
I served him faithfully,
I obeyed him in every way.

Then one day,
he took me to Cikupa.
Everyone knew him there.
He was not only a road-worker
but a pimp as well.

As if I were bewitched,
I enjoyed love and suffering.
I obeyed him completely.
I was his favorite girl.
Truck drivers fought over me.

I made him a tidy fortune.
We went to Karawaci,
Cimone, Cikupa and Balaraja.
In Cilegon the men queued up for me.

The highways from Karawaci to Merak
were part of our national development project.
Young women from poor villages
found employment in roadside brothels.

Factories and brothels belong together.
Koreans, German and Japanese men,
I've tasted them all.
In Cilegon
I contracted syphilis for the first time.

I fought the disease.
There were plenty of medicines.
And when I was better
my boss took me to Ancol in Jakarta.

Jakarta, oh Jakarta!
Neon lamps like trees.
Roads filled with cars and buses, like rivers!
Clean, rich customers.
Breakfasts in restaurants every day.
Waking up late and going shopping.

It was like a dream.
Without any foundation.
Much happened.
None of it affected me.
I drifted along through various experiences
and had no control over anything.

Any thoughts of you, my darling,
were quickly forgotten.
I buried my shame deep inside me.
I survived one attack of syphilis after another.
Then one day I caught a high fever
and my bones seemed to break inside me.
Since then, I have never been cured.
I have sudden headaches.
I feel weak.
Cancer of the womb.
Repeated vaginitis.

I was broken goods,
Worth very little.
A cheap slut.
I moved on to Kalideres,
Muara Angke, Tanah Abang, Bongkaran,
and Jati Petamburan.

Even though I was almost dead
I was protected in those places.
They are garbage dumps.
I mixed with them all.
Toadstools growing in dark caves.
Consoling grubby men
as they pretended to forget their poverty.
Finally, my darling,
I was banished to Kalijodo.
Without a house.
Without my health.
Without any protection.

And now, tonight,
perched beside the highway,
facing towards our village,
I feel as though I'm floating
in the darkness.
I feel disoriented, ready to die,
drained of energy.
The world is vanishing.
All sorts of memories pass by.
Unexpectedly, I see your face too.

I feel a warmth in my forehead.
I want to sing you
a decayed love song
with my silent, blue, dumb, open mouth.

Darling, you are like a god.
Glorious and very far away.
Forgive me, I have sinned.
My song, darling,
wants to hover on the tops of the bamboo bushes.
And cannot.
It is stolen by the noisy passing trucks.

When my song finishes, darling,
I will die.

Indonesia, May 1998: A Poem

I am writing this poem in the dark days of kings.
Bleeding bodies spread out on the highways.
Undirected anger everywhere.
Fear rising from the garbage of our lives.
Confused thoughts beating against the knots of history.

A mad age!
A dark night of inhuman thought!
The pavilions of belief torn apart
The law books shredded in the gutters.
Life's certainties staggering in the sewers.

Power's multicolored illusions.
The magical light of kings' crowns.
From the time of Abraham and Moses
God has always reminded us
that the law must stand above the desires
of politicians, kings and soldiers.

Chaos emerges from the mists of fear!
Despair clashes with bayonets!
Stop hoping for the Righteous King!
There is no Messiah. The Just King is a lie!
We must create the Rule of Law.

The Rule of Law is our polestar in the storm.
The bitter smell of blood fills the air.
It is our witness and says:
When the government betrays the sovereignty of the people,
when carpetbaggers defile the national economy,
when peacekeepers betray peace,
the oppressed people will be ready to imitate their rulers,
they will become tyrants in the marketplaces and highways.

Oh, lords of a transitory world!
Oh, citizens bewildered by power!
How can you be so blind and deaf?
How can you deceive yourselves?
When you refuse to think rationally
you open the doors for dark thoughts
to emerge from every chaotic corner!

The face of the Motherland is covered
with a veil of despair.
Her tears flow from my poem.

It is Time

It is time
to take off your shoes
covered with stories
to put down your backpack
filled with problems
and wash away your misfortune
to calm your worried soul.

Anger and sorrow
become a sea of hatred, balls of fire,
uncontrollably slamming against the self
weakening our resistance.
Resistance is not destructive,
it is necessary
if we are to do good.

It is time
to put down our sabers and rifles,
to eat plain soup
cleanse your system,
drink herbal tea,
to look at the trees
through an open window.

Misspoken words
can be explained and corrected.
But when weapons are wrongly used
the consequences are serious.
And when lives are lost,
how can you change that?

It is time
to sit and talk together.
To honor each other as human beings.
To read the record
of the human heart
to remember the world to come.
Ahimsa,
non-violence
in the service of common dignity.
Anekanta,
truth is relative,
understand and implement
diversity in human existence
in the same way
that nature is multiple.

Accept a common life,
despite our many differences.
Reach agreement
not for the sake of uniformity
but as a basis for working together
in the service of truth.

Aparigraha,
non-covetousness
each side taking off its uniforms
and badges of rank
so they can sit together.
Each side acknowledging
its commitment to truth.

It is time
to appreciate the beauty of butterflies.
Flowers in the forest.
The softness of a mother's breast.
For tomorrow's grandchildren
to find inspiration
in history.

It is time,
It is time.
Yes, my brothers and sisters.
It is time for all of us.
To embrace the moon,
shining above the three mountains.

Don't Be Afraid, Mother!

The sun must rise.
The sun must set.
Breast cancer, rheumatism,
and gray hairs,
are all part of our transitory lives.

There are governors dining on the bodies of factory workers.
There are regional heads eating asphalt,
schoolchildren becoming dwarves.
Don't be afraid, Mother!
We must endure.
Fear only increases oppression.
People are born.
People die.
Between your birth and future death
atomic bombs fell on Hiroshima and Nagasaki,
Japanese soldiers
beheaded Asian patriots,
members of the Klu Klux Klan
lit fires to black churches,
an American terrorist set off a bomb in Oklahoma
burning old people, women and children,
European tourists have been robbed and murdered in Miami,
English soldiers killed teenagers in Ireland,
Irish rebels exploded bombs in nervous London.

Don't be afraid, Mother!
Don't let them shout at you.
Don't let them threaten you.
Fear makes oppression worse.

Time's river carries away the grief of withered dreams.
The sweat of the earth that supports human civilization
has been turned into uranium and mercury.
Don't be afraid, Mother!
The moon is like an eyebrow,
let it rise in your heart.
The Milky Way chants God's name across your forehead.
I kiss your hand, Mother.
Your womb and breasts are a source of hope.
The source of human power
from one age to another.

Where are You Now, De'Na? *)

Eventually the news reached me:
A tsunami wave, 23 meters high,
had smashed your house.
Leaving only broken fragments.
Where are you, De'Na?
I tried to phone you
many times.
How are you, Acheh?
I saw the bodies on television
sprawled in the streets.
Towns and villages destroyed.
Nature angry
people in pain
and anguish.

Where are you now, De'Na?
When the tsunami hit your house,
were you doing your morning exercises
was your widowed mother
cleaning the bathroom?

De'Na, we have no choice
about life and death.

---

*) De'Na was an arts worker in Acheh, whom Rendra met in August 2004 at the Fourth
   Acheh Arts Festival. Although his house was flattened in the tsunami of December 26,
   2004, De'Na survived. (See Fikar W Eda 2005.)

But death and loss
always bring sorrow
to those who remain.
With sorrow comes the questions:
why did this happen
and why did it happen to me?

Humans have rights, De'Na,
but nature has more.
My deep sorrow
struggles with nature.
My questions about fate
slowly crawl around a silent lonely world.

De'Na! De'Na!
Now you are part
of this deep dark mystery.
Grief, anger and frailty
make my life fragile.
Without purity
how can our lives
make peace
with death?

De'Na, my heart screams in its grief.
Where are you? How are you?
I cannot push away that image,
whether my eyes are open or closed,
the picture of people running
pursued by a 23 meter wave.
And the earthquake
that drowned tall buildings,

shattered highways,
ripped open deep ravines.
Thousands of people
were reduced to rubbish
by the storm.

Nature is awesome, De'Na!
This was no ordinary form of death!
It makes me tremble!
What does culture mean
if we do not know this?
What does poetry mean?
Life and struggle have meaning
only when we recognize our limitations.

De'Na,
are you smiling
as you read this poem?

Maskumambang *)

Day slowly breaks.
A *bintaro* blossom falls
in the library yard.
I sit on a rock
beside the pond
near the taro bushes,
weeping.

Oh my grandchildren!
What sort of an age, what sort of civilization,
are we leaving you?
My soul offers you this *maskumambang*.

We are the ignorant generation.
We live beyond our means.
We do not know how
to plan for the future.

Because we do not know
how to read the past,
and do not know
how to read the present,
our plans for the future
are based on idle speculations
and empty dreams.

---

*) A traditional Javanese verse form lamenting the power of illusion.

Oh my grandchildren!
The nation is overwhelmed by an age gone mad.
Our plans for future wellbeing are thrown about in confusion,
we wearily cling to rocks.
But I still insist
on reason and conscience,
even if they only exist in the gutter these days.

Our people are like dice
caught in a can full of debt,
shaken about by powerful nations
we cannot resist.
All done in the name of development,
economic strategies we have learned
from our colonial masters.

They taught us how to run the state
and administer the law
in their way.
The people and the law
have no sovereignty of their own.
The right to rule belongs
to the government and political parties.

Oh spiteful civilization!
The nation's dignity lies in shreds.

The state quarrels.
The people are weak.
Arbitrary force rules.
Markets are set alight.
Villages are burned.

Tramps' huts destroyed,
with no recompense provided.
All in the superstitious name of development.
Restaurants are burned.
Shops burned.
Churches burned.
In the name of religious revival.

When religion plays politics
it begins to decay!
Politics has no head.
No ears. No heart.
It only knows victory and defeat.
Allies and enemies.
Shallow civilization.

We need politics to live as a nation
but politics must not corrupt
faith and intelligence,
the rule of reason.

Human sovereignty,
our common life in this world,
must protect the sovereignty of nature,
the sovereignty of human society,
and the sovereignty of reason.

The sun slowly rises in the east
past the *jinjing* trees.
The friendly air caresses my body.
I can smell onions frying in the kitchen.

Two bees buzz
making love in the sky.
"Mas Willy!" my wife calls.
She can see that I have been crying.
I stand, ready to talk.
"Hush, be quiet!" she whispers.
"Don't cry. Write a poem.
Don't talk."

God, I Love You

I am frail
but determined
I am sick and ache
but I don't need help.

I want to drink rice-water
I am never short of breath
but my body is no longer suited
to holding natural postures.

I want to cleanse my body
of poisonous chemicals.

I want to go back to natural ways.
I want to serve God better.

God, I love you.

Sources

BB	*Blues Untuk Bonnie.* PT Dunia Pustaka Jaya,1971	NJ	*Nyanyian dari Jalanan* (in EKS). PT Pembangunan, 1961
BOT	*Ballada Orang-Orang Tercinta.* PT Pembangunan, 1957	NOU	*Nyanyian Orang Urakan.* Mangap Studio, 1985
DAC	*Doa untuk Anak Cucu.* PT Bentang Pustaka, Yogyakarta, 2013	OR	*Orang-Orang Rangkasbitung.* PT Dunia Pustaka Jaya, 1990
DOA	*Disebabkan Oleh Angin.* PT Dunia Pustaka Jaya, 1993	PBA	*Perjalanan Bu Aminah.* Yayasan Obor Indonesia, 1997
EKS	*Empat Kumpulan Sajak.* PT Pembangunan, 1961	PPdP	*Potret Pembangunan dalam Puisi.* Lembaga Studi Pembangunan, 1980
KK	*Kakawin Kawin* (in EKS). PT Pembangunan, 1961	SDP	*Sajak-sajak Duabelas Perak* (in EKS). PT Pembangunan, 1961
MB	*Mencari Bapa.* Yayasan Obor Indonesia, 1997	SST	*Sajak-Sajak Sepatu Tua.* PT Dunia Pustaka Jaya, 1972
MS	*Malam Stanza* (in EKS). PT Pembangunan, 1961		

The Translators

HA Harry Aveling   JM John H McGlynn   BR Burton Raffel

No.	English Title	Original Title	Written	Source	Translator
1	Flowers Fall	Bunga Gugur	1954	MB	HA
2.	Ballad of Kasan and Patima	Ballada Kasan dan Patima	1955	BOT	HA
3.	Ballad of the Death of Atmo Karpo	Ballada Terbunuhnya Atmo Karpo	1955	BOT	HA
4.	Guerrilla	Gerilya	1955	BOT	HA
5.	Prisoner	Tahanan	1955	BOT	HA
6.	The Stubborn Child	Anak yang Angkuh	1955	BOT	HA
7.	Woman Waiting	Perempuan yang Menunggu	1956	MS	BR
8.	Black River	Kali Hitam	1956	MS	BR
9.	Black Eyes	Mata Hitam	1956	MS	BR

No.	English Title	Original Title	Written	Source	Translator
10.	Black Rocks	Batu Hitam	1957	MS	BR
11.	Scorched Earth	Bumi Hangus	1957	MS	BR
12.	Violet Serenade	Serenada Violet	1957	KK	BR
13.	Ostankino Church	Gereja Ostankino, Moskwa	1957	SST	BR
14.	Green Serenade	Serenada Hijau	1958	KK	BR
15.	Lullaby for a Bride	Nina Bobo bagi Pengantin	1958	KK	BR
16.	White Serenade	Serenada Putih	1959	KK	BR
17.	Love Letter	Surat Cinta	1959	KK	BR
18.	Episode	Episode	1959	KK	BR
19.	Invitation	Undangan	1959	KK	BR
20.	The Moon's Bed	Ranjang Bulan, Ranjang Pengantin	1959	KK	BR
21.	The Moscow River	Sungai Moskwa	1959	SST	BR
22.	Aichun Hotel, Canton	Hotel Aichung, Canton	1959	SST	BR
23.	A Saint	Amsal Seorang Santu	1959	SST	HA
24.	Prayer of the Hungry	Doa Orang lapar	1959	SST	HA
25.	Rose Psalm	Masmur Mawar	1959	SST	HA
26.	The World's First Face	Wajah Dunia yang Pertama	1960	KK	BR
27.	Knife in the Road	Pisau di Jalan	1960	ND	BR
28.	Hotel International, Pyongyang	Hotel Internasional, Pyongyang	1960	SST	BR
29.	Morning Psalm	Masmur Pagi	1960	SST	HA
30.	Evening Prayer	Doa Malam	1960	SST	HA
31.	An Angry World	Sebuah Dunia yang Marah	1960	SST	HA
32	A Soldier's Prayer Before Battle	Doa Seorang Serdadu Sebelum Berperang	1960	SST	HA
33.	An Old Man's Poem for His Wife	Sajak Seorang Tua untuk Istrinya	1960	SST	HA
34.	I Call Your Name	Kupanggili Namamu	1964	BB	HA
35.	For MG	Kepada MG	1964	BB	JM
36.	Blues for Bonnie	Blues untuk Bonnie	1964	BB	JM
37.	Rick from Corona	Rick dari Corona	1966	BB	JM
38.	A Worldly Song	Nyanyian Duniawi	1966	BB	HA
39.	Testimony, 1967	Kesaksian Tahun 1967	1967	BB	HA

No.	English Title	Original Title	Written	Source	Translator
40.	Twilight View	Pemandangan Senjakala	1967	BB	HA
41.	Prostitutes of Jakarta Unite!	Bersatulah Pelacur-Pelacur Kota Jakarta	1967	BB	HA
42.	A Pickpocket's Advice to His Mistress	Pesan Pencopet kepada Pacarnya	1967	BB	HA
43.	Swan Song	Nyanyian Angsa	1967	BB	HA
44	Sermon	Khotbah	1967	BB	HA
45.	Suto's Song for Fatima	Nyanyian Suto untuk Fatima	1968	BB	HA
46.	Fatima's Song for Suto	Nyanyian Fatima untuk Suto	1968	BB	HA
47.	A Poem About Condors	Sajak Burung-burung Kondor	1973	PPdP	HA
48.	I Hear the Sound	Aku Mendengar Suara	1975	PPdP	HA
49.	A Pile of Corn	Sajak Seonggok Jagung	1975	PPdP	JM
50.	A Poem About a Girl And Her Employer	Sajak Gadis dan Majikan	1975	PPdP	HA
51.	A Poem About a Family Photograph	Sajak Potret Keluarga	1975	PPdP	HA
52.	A Poem for a Student Meeting	Sajak Pertemuan Mahasiswa	1977	PPdP	HA
53.	A Poem About a Bottle of Beer	Sajak Sebotol Bir	1977	PPdP	HA
54.	A Poem About Bali	Sajak Pulau Bali	1977	PPdP	HA
55.	A Poem for Joki Tobing From Widuri	Sajak Joki Tobing untuk Widuri	1977	PPdP	JM
56.	A Poem for Widuri from Joki Tobing	Sajak Widuri untuk Joki Tobing	1977	PPdP	JM
57.	A Poem About Old Friends	Sajak Kenalan Lamamu	1977	PPdP	HA
58.	A Poem About a Guerrilla	Lagu Seorang Gerilya	1977	PPdP	HA
59.	A Poem by an Old Man Under a Tree	Sajak Seorang Tua di Bawah Pohon	1977	PPdP	HA
60.	A Poem about Eyes	Sajak Mata-mata	1978	PPdP	HA
61.	Poor People	Orang-Orang Miskin	1978	PPdP	HA
62.	An Angry Poem	Sajak Orang Kepanasan	1979	NOU	HA
63.	A Bat	Kelelawar	1981	NOU	HA
64.	New Year's Poem, 1990	Sajak Tahun Baru 1990	1989	OR	JM

No.	English Title	Original Title	Written	Source	Translator
65.	An Old Man's Poem about Bandung, "A Sea of Fire"	Sajak Seorang Tua tentang Bandung Lautan Api	1989	PBA	HA
66.	For the People of Rangkasbitung	Demi Orang-Orang Rangkasbitung	1990	OR	HA
67.	Saijah's Song for Adinda	Nyanyian Saijah untuk Adinda	1991	OR	HA
68.	Adinda's Song for Saijah	Nyanyian Adinda untuk Saijah	1991	OR	HA
69.	Indonesia, May 1998: A Poem	Sajak Bulan Mei 1998 di Indonesia	1998	DAC	HA
70.	It is Time	Inilah Saatnya	2001	DAC	HA
71.	Don't Be Afraid, Mother!	Jangan Takut, Ibu!	2003	DAC	HA
72.	Where are You Now, De'Na?	Di Mana kamu, De'Na?	2004	DAC	HA
73.	Maskumambang	Maskumambang	2006	DAC	HA
74.	God, I Love You	Tuhan, Aku Cinta PadaMu	2009	DAC	HA

The Author

Willibrordus Surendra Bhawana Rendra Brotoatmojo (November 7, 1935-August 6, 2009), widely known as WS Rendra or just "Rendra", was one of Indonesia's most popular playwrights and poets but is equally renowned for his political activism. Born in Surakarta, Central Java, Rendra's father was a teacher of Indonesian and Old Javanese and his mother a classical Javanese dancer.

After studying English literature and culture at Gadjah Mada University in Yogyakarta, he moved to the United States in 1964 to study drama at the American Academy of Dramatic Arts. Together with his wife Sunarti and Azwar AN, he established the Bengkel Teater upon his return to Indonesia in August 1967. The company's dramatic productions soon became the benchmark for success in the world of modern Indonesian drama.

In 1970 he converted from Catholicism to Islam and changed his first two names to "Wahyu Sulaiman" (the Inspiration of Solomon)— which he continued to abbreviate as "WS"—but then later dropped those names altogether and went simply by the name "Rendra". When he changed his religion, he also took a new wife, Sitoresmi, a former dramatic student. In 1976, he married again, this time to Ken Zuraida. (Sitoresmi requested and was granted a divorce in 1979. Sunarti followed suit in 1982.) He had eleven children from his three marriages.

Bengkel Teater productions, including their interpretations of both classical Western plays and Indonesian stories, had a profound influence on modern Indonesian theater. His poems—read and performed for huge audiences throughout the archipelago—had a similar impact on the development of Indonesian poetry during the years of the New Order government (1965-1998). During this time, Rendra was one of the few creative people who had the courage to openly express dissent. His poetry readings became occasions for mass public protest throughout the 1970s and 1980s.

In April 1978, during a poetry reading at the Ismail Marzuki Arts Center in Jakarta, government agents threw ammonia bombs on to the stage to disrupt his performance. Three days later, they took him into custody for "reasons of public safety" and held him, without trial, for five months. He was released only on the condition that he refrain from performing poetry or drama—which he did until 1986, when he wrote, directed and starred in his eight hour long play, *Panembahan Reso*. The play discussed the issue of the succession of presidential leadership—a subject that was taboo at that time.

After the fall of the Soeharto government in 1998 and the beginning of democratization, Rendra remained a dominant figure in the emerging world of modern Indonesian literature and theater and became the patron of an unrestricted, free and socially engaged artistic community. The number of awards he received during his lifetime is very extensive.

Other Contributors

Edi Haryono was born in Pekalongan in 1954. After completing high school at the SMA Muhammadiyah he moved to Yogyakarta, joining Rendra's Bengkel Teater in 1974. For a period of twelve years, he served as an organizer for the company and script archivist, acting in each production through to *Panembahan Reso* in 1986. He has written prize-winning short stories and edited a number of books by and on Rendra, including *Memberi Makna Pada Hidup Yang Fana* (Giving Meaning to Our Brief Life, essays, 1999), published by Pabelan Jayakarta, Jakarta; and *Rendra dan Teater Modern Indonesia* (Rendra and Modern Indonesian Theater, 2000), *Ketika Rendra Baca Sajak* (When Rendra Reads Poetry, 2004) and *Membaca Kepenyairan Rendra* (Reading Rendra's Poetics, 2005), all published by Kepel Press, Yogyakarta.

Harry Aveling has translated extensively from Indonesian and Malay literature. His recent translations include *Morphology of Desire* (Lontar, Jakarta 2013) and *A Body Only A Body*, (Penerbit Waktoe, Magelang 2013) both by Dorothea Rosa Herliany; *A Borrowed Body* (Lontar, Jakarta 2015) by Joko Pinurbo; *A History of Classical Malay Literature* by Liaw Yock Fang (translated with Razif Bahari, Obor, Jakarta and ISEAS, Singapore 2013); and *A Treasury of Devotion: Sant Charandas's Bhaktipadarth* (co-translated from Hindi with Peter Friedlander, Prestige, Delhi 2014). He was Visiting Professor of English in Creative Writing at the University of Maryland during the Fall Semester 2014.

John H McGlynn, originally from Wisconsin, the United States, is a long-term resident of Indonesia, having lived in Jakarta almost continually since 1976. A graduate of the University of Michigan Ann Arbor, he is the translator of several dozen publications, both under his own name and his penname, Willem Samuels. Through the Lontar Foundation, which he established with four Indonesian authors in 1987, he has edited, overseen the translation of, and published more than 150 books on Indonesian literature and culture. Also through the Lontar Foundation, he initiated the "On the Record" film documentation program which has thus far produced twenty-four films on Indonesian writers and more than thirty films on Indonesian performance traditions. As a film subtitler, he has subtitled more than 100 Indonesian films.

Burton Raffel (born 1928), an American poet, educator, and translator, is best known to scholars of Indonesia for having introduced modern Indonesian poetry to the English-language reading public. He first came to Indonesia as a Ford Foundation fellow in 1953, and taught English in Makassar until 1955. After familiarizing himself with the history of Indonesian poetry, he edited *An Anthology of Modern Indonesian Poetry*, published by the University of California Press in 1964, and authored *The Development of Modern Indonesian Poetry*, containing translations of poems by a score of Indonesian poets, published by SUNY Press in 1967. In 1970, he published *The Complete Poetry and Prose of Chairil Anwar*, also with SUNY Press (republished by Ohio University Press in 1993).